Fostering Creativity in Self and the Organization

Fostering Creativity in Self and the Organization

Your Professional Edge

Eric W. Stein

Fostering Creativity in Self and the Organization:
Your Professional Edge

First published in 2014 by
Business Expert Press, LLC
222 East 46th Street, New York, NY 10017
www.businessexpertpress.com

ISBN-13: 978-1-60649-798-2 (paperback)
ISBN-13: 978-1-60649-799-9 (e-book)

Business Expert Press Human Resource Management and Organizational Behavior Collection

Collection ISSN: 1946-5637 (print)
Collection ISSN: 1946-5645 (electronic)

Cover and interior design by Exeter Premedia Services Private Ltd., Chennai, India

First edition: 2014

10 9 8 7 6 5 4 3 2 1

Printed in the United States of America.

I dedicate this book to the memory of my parents Lou and Irene Stein, who were both improvisers. My father was a great jazz pianist who played with the likes of Charlie Parker and many other jazz luminaries. We discussed many of these ideas over the years. My mother and father together improvised the business of living and raising a family together.

Abstract

The focus of this book is how to maximize your creative potential both professionally and personally. A central theme of this book is that successful creative expression is a function of hard work and discipline rather than innate talent or genius. Reaching your creative potential requires an open mind. To begin, we discuss some of mental models that facilitate or impede your development as a creative person. The book also identifies specific ways a person can accelerate his or her progress as a creative person.

Since creativity encompasses so many things, we focus on four creative behaviors and cognitions critical to self-development and career advancement: *improvisation capacity, design thinking, your experimental and scientific mind,* and *aesthetic awareness.* These abilities are critical success factors for 21st century professionals.

I illustrate how to leverage these abilities along with innate strengths derived from your multiple intelligence inventory, which include linguistic intelligence, mathematical/logical intelligence, visual/spatial intelligence, musical intelligence, interpersonal intelligence, intrapersonal intelligence, kinesthetic intelligence, and naturalistic intelligence. The book concludes with a plan of action to systematically develop your creative potential over time.

Keywords

creativity, career management, personal development, improvisation, design, experimentation, aesthetics, learning, leadership, management, worldviews, mental models, IQ, intelligence, strengths

Contents

Preface

Imagination is the beginning of creation. You imagine what you desire, you will what you imagine and at last you create what you will.
—George Bernard Shaw, writer

This book is about developing individual creativity for personal satisfaction and career advancement. For those interested in building creative high-power teams and organizations, the reader is referred to *Designing Creative High Power Teams and Organizations: Beyond Leadership*, which is also available through Business Expert Press.

Creativity is a broad subject and may be explored in many different ways. In this book I pay most attention to four specific *behaviors* and *cognitions* associated with creativity: improvisation, design, experimentation, and aesthetics. My fundamental premise is that all of us are creative in some way and have the ability to produce things new and innovative. Everyone. Creativity is not just the province of artists, musicians, and writers. We all have creative talents and can learn the behaviors associated with creativity. We can *choose* to adopt the role of creator; it is not something we are born with. By the time you finish this book I hope to convince you of this point.

Acknowledgments

Writing a book is a journey and you meet many, many people along the way. Some are old friends and are familiar. Others may be new or transient. Some people you meet in person and others you meet on the written page. Each of these people contributes in various ways to what ultimately appears between the covers of a book. Sometimes it is a subtle thought. Other times it may be a direct contribution like finding references or sharing quotations. All become grist for the creative writer's mill.

I would like to thank Maureen Benner for pursuing an independent study with me, which allowed me to teach her much of this material on a one-on-one basis. Her questions and comments helped to sharpen my thinking. She also helped to organize components of the bibliography as well as synthesize several of my ideas into tables that I think add value for the reader.

Many of these ideas first appeared in a class I taught several years ago at Penn State. I am indebted to my students who wrestled with this material with me. I also would like to acknowledge Penn State for allowing me to teach a class such as this that does not fit easily into an MBA course category.

To the reviewers of my first complete draft of part of this work, I express my gratitude. My sincere thanks to Chris Johannessen, Maureen Benner, Paul Hilt, Andrea Laine, and Victoria McMahon for constructive criticism, suggestions, and feedback on elements of the book. Thanks to Paul Hilt for his time and insight regarding these ideas through our discussions over the years. Special appreciation for Anne Calbazana for her support and enthusiasm for the project, especially in the later stages.

I owe a special thanks to Joy Field of Boston College. Our casual conversation between sessions at the NE Decision Sciences Institute conference led me to Scott Isenberg of Business Expert Press. Scott has been terrific to work with and I thank him for getting my proposal to the right people at Business Expert Press. Special thanks to David Parker for giving this project the green light.

To the musicians, writers, entrepreneurs, and artists, who have inspired me with their creations I owe a debt of gratitude: Miles Davis, Paul Desmond, Stan Getz, Steve Jobs, Jeff Bezos, Frank Gehry, Isaac Asimov, and many others. I owe special thanks to jazz pianist, mentor, friend, and father, Lou Stein. We spent many hours exploring the creative mind, improvisation, listening to music, and just plain having fun. Thanks Dad.

Finally, the publication of this book marks a milestone on an intellectual journey but not an end. I have set up a website, ideasmethod.com, to provide additional resources and hopefully to facilitate future discussion on these interesting topics and to grow a community of practice. To all who have and will contribute to these conversations, I thank you for your ideas and input.

CHAPTER 1

The Big Picture

Creativity is the ability to introduce order into the randomness of nature.

> —Eric Hoffer, American social writer and
> philosopher, 1902–1983

Leaders are expected to lead under a variety of conditions, from boom to bust. However, it takes a special type of leader, and cast of characters, to produce innovative new products and services. Steve Jobs of Apple Computer had a track record of identifying the talent to produce game-changing products and services: the Macintosh, iTunes, the iPod, the iPhone, and the iPad. He led the effort, but it was the designers and engineers, who built these devices. We are interested in how the latter think. There are hundreds of books on leadership, and while we will discuss leadership in certain creative contexts, this is not a book on leadership. It is not a book on management either. It is a book on creation and production. The Greek word for this activity is *Poiesis*, which means to create or to make.

Consequently, we will focus primarily on the role of the creator in the innovation process. This is not to say that the roles of manager and leader are not important; they are and I will highlight the importance of those roles where it is appropriate. However, given the goals of this book, we will focus on how to reach your potential as a creator, designer, experimenter, and improviser in personal and organizational contexts, and refer you to resources that cover the managerial and leadership dimensions of the process.

How Creativity Relates to Business

Consider the primary ways that businesses compete. The generic competitive strategies were best articulated by Michael Porter in the 1980s. In his model, a firm either assumes overall cost leadership or differentiation.[1] Cost leadership requires paying attention to businesses processes and resource management. Differentiation requires attention to marketing and enhancing the overall *value* of the product or service. This could be increasing the *quality, aesthetics, functionality,* or *flexibility* of the product or service.

These are the very things that require creative thinking to nurture and to deliver. What kinds of creative thinking? To differentiate products and services requires an understanding of aesthetics, which concerns itself with an appreciation of form (from the perspective of the consumer). Aesthetics goes hand in hand with design, which considers both form and function (from the perspective of the designer). By function, we mean, "What kind of experience is created for the user?" To best understand users, you need to live among them, understand them, and *empathize* with them. What do they really need and want? How can that value be delivered? To really understand a client, you need to rethink your interaction; that is, you need to think like a modern-day ethnographer. Designing great products and services requires flexibility, adaptability, and the ability to *improvise* and *experiment*. Great design companies learn from their mistakes (even revere them) and move on to the next iteration of the product or service. They take risks.

So this book is about teaching you a new set of skills that enable you to differentiate yourself, and consequently, your organization in terms of its products or services; that is, its value proposition. To do that, we need to reformulate ourselves as creators and designers. We need to adopt new skills related to design, aesthetics, improvisation, and experimentation. We need to transform ourselves in order to transform the world around us.

The IDEAS Method

Although it is as much a philosophy as a method, a quick way to remember the essential skills of 21st-century professionals identified in this book is to simply remember the word: IDEAS (Figure 1.1). IDEAS stand for:

- **I**mprovisation
- **D**esign
- **E**xperimentation
- **A**esthetics
- **S**trengths

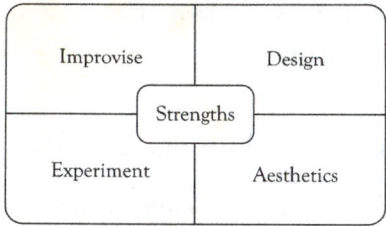

Figure 1.1 Components of the IDEAS method

Improvisation is the ability to make effective real-time decisions in new and complex situations using current information and appropriately chosen (or modified) routines, scripts, and patterns.

Design is the ability to envision and construct an object or process that meets the goals and requirements of a particular user.

Experimentation is the ability of an observer to decide between two competing goals, courses of action, or viewpoints by designing a process that yields sufficient information to rank each choice according to certain criteria. This process is often referred to as an *experiment*.

Aesthetic awareness is the ability to discriminate between various sensory inputs (e.g., visual, auditory, etc.), recognize the feelings and thoughts invoked, and to rank the object of reflection in terms of certain criteria such as beauty.

Strengths pertain to the multiple intelligences possessed by all people that can be targeted for development and creative expression.

My goal, therefore, is to share with you ways to increase your improvisational capacity, develop your design proficiency, practice experimentation, expand your aesthetic awareness, and to leverage your strengths.

Developing IDEAS Using PPP (P3)

Developing proficiency and depth in each component of the IDEAS model is accomplished through discipline and hard work. However it is much easier to break this process into three sub processes:

- **P**reparation
- **P**ractice
- **P**erformance

We prepare. We practice. We perform. Each chapter discusses development using the P3 framework.

Who Should Read This Book?

This book is a method of transformation for any individual. It is suitable for managers, leaders, creative people, as well as graduate and advanced undergraduate students. It addresses the following needs:

- You want to identify and capitalize on your cognitive and emotional strengths.
- You want to develop your creative talents.
- You want to invigorate your career or make a career change.
- You want to understand how to make real-time decisions more effectively.
- You want to learn to become an improviser, a designer, or both.
- You want to accelerate your development through exploratory learning.
- You want to immerse yourself in flow and develop your aesthetic awareness.
- You want to develop the creative potential of your people.

For faculty, it can also be used as a textbook or supplemental text for a class on creativity and personal development.

How to Use This Book

It is very difficult to teach creative thinking. This book is meant to be used in conjunction with other resources and activities in the following contexts:

- Self-study and development
- In a corporate training class
- In an organization undergoing change or transformation
- In a university class on creativity and innovation

Some of ideas of the book are dense and not assimilated immediately. It will take some time to absorb, comprehend, and later apply these ideas in the workplace or your personal life. The ideas benefit most from reflection[2] and conversations with other people engaged in the pursuit of similar knowledge and by applying the ideas in the field. The Ideas Method™ website (ideasmethod.com) provides additional resources for development.

Assumptions About Learning and Development

Learning takes place in a variety of ways. We learn through books, by talking to other people, and by doing. Learning can simply be the acquisition of knowledge as if we are containers to be filled. On the other hand, learning can occur at much deeper level and can be much less passive. This book is predicated on a *constructivist* approach to learning. Constructivism assumes that learners take an active role in what they learn. They are not simply passively waiting for information to be dumped into them. The information may not be presented in clean, bite-sized pieces as is common in the worlds of journalism and television. Part of learning is about constructing meaning from seemingly disparate data, information, and experience.

Social constructivism argues that learning takes place through our active interpretation of experience. Sharing that experience with others helps learners to create meaning and to construct models of how the world works. The role of the teacher, or the writer, is to provide opportunities to learn in this way. A well-known cognitive psychologist and educator observed: "Knowledge is not passively received but actively built up..."[3]

Furthermore, learners participate in the construction of models of the world in which they operate, both personal and professional. People employ a "cycle of theory-prediction-test-failure-accommodation-new theory" to test their ideas, which give rise to socially agreed upon rules, patterns, and language.[4] In short, we put forth our personal theories, test them, share them with other people, and over time they become accepted into the patterns of social interaction; that is, we learn. It is best that you interact with these ideas actively and in conjunction with others with similar aims. It will accelerate the learning process.

To recap, this book assumes that you, the reader, are actively partici-
pating in the construction of meaning and theories-in-use[5] (i.e., models)
about the world. Participation, experimentation, conversation, and sense-
making are essential skills that are critical to self-development and creative expression.

Chapter Summary

Learning to become a creative person requires patience and discipline
much more so than innate talent or genius. While there are many ways
to exhibit your creative talents and in many disciplines, we will focus
on the cultivation of four general skill areas: improvisational capacity,
design proficiency, your experimental and scientific mind, and aesthetic
awareness. A simple way to remember these things is to think of the word
IDEAS. In essence, you will augment your creative abilities along with
your natural strengths. Developing as a creative person requires that you
rethink your assumptions about yourself and others. Dedication and
hard work are the foundations of the creative mind. Whenever possible,
each chapter highlights ways to prepare, practice, and perform, which I
refer to as P3. I assume throughout this process that you will be active in
your own development. As you attempt new things, you will construct
meaning in order to reach the next level of development.

CHAPTER 2

Know Your Worldview

Mental models are the images, assumptions, and stories which we carry in our minds of ourselves, other people, institutions, and every aspect of the world.

—Peter Senge, organizational theorist

If we are to change our world view, images have to change. The artist now has a very important job to do. He's not a little peripheral figure entertaining rich people, he's really needed.

—David Hockney, artist

Creatures of a very particular making, we need to know the cultural blinders that narrow our world view as well as the psychological blinders that narrow our view of our personal experience.

—Christina Baldwin, author

Overview

To become effective creators, we need to understand ourselves because our beliefs and assumptions ultimately end up in our creations. We all operate under certain core assumptions about ourselves, the world, and the places we work and play. To effect change and to be most effective in organizations, or in life for that matter, you and others around you need to examine your core assumptions and, if need be, modify them. In this chapter, we examine how the core beliefs we hold shape the world we inhabit, the world we design, and the world we interact in.

Constructing a Worldview

We develop many, many core assumptions as we gain experience in life. These contribute to what is often referred to as our "worldview." A worldview is composed of one or more "*mental models.*" Our mental models are based on the knowledge gained from experiences we have in life. For example, we develop mental models of the world of work, romance, sports, family, change, and so forth. Mental models are often built on a base of rules such as, "If the mole looks suspicious, then see a doctor." More subtly, we develop complex assumptions about our brains, interactions between and among people, the physical world, and about change.

The concept of a worldview has a long history and it is outside the scope of this work to explore it fully. It first appeared in Kant's "Critique of Judgment" published in 1790 as the concept of *Weltanschauung*, or worldview.[1] It has been used by religious scholars to emphasize elements that explicitly connect human beings to God and by secularists to better understand politics, economics, culture, science, and ethics. From a pragmatic perspective, a worldview represents answers to a series of questions that help us to make choices. There are five key questions that any worldview should address (Table 2.1).[2]

Table 2.1 Key components of any worldview[3]

#	Model	Questions[4]
1	Description of the World ("What?")	• What is the nature of our world? • How is it structured, and how does it function?
2	Explanation of the World ("Why?")	• Why is our world the way it is and not different? • Why are we the way we are and not different? • What kind of global explanatory principles can we put forward?
3	Evaluation of the World ("Value?")	• Why do we feel the way we feel in this world? • How do we assess global reality and the role of our species in it?
4	Action in the World ("How?")	• How are we to act and to create in this world? • How and in what different ways can we influence the world and transform it? • What are the general principles by which we should organize our actions?
5	Future of the World ("How?")	• What future is open to us in this world? • By what criteria are we to select these possible futures? • How do we get from our current state to the future?

Having a *complete* set of answers to all or even some of these questions is an ideal. Most likely, you have partial answers to some of these questions. One of the goals of this book is to help you to find answers to some of these questions and, if need be, modify your answers to match your goals. If you are truly interested in developing as a creator, then it is important to know whether your views help or hinder you in this regard.

Expanding Your Mental Models and Worldview

There are many aspects to the world that we live in. We live in a physical world that is governed by certain laws and principles. We inhabit bodies that are subject to certain constraints and limitations. We also have constructed and live in an elaborate social world within which we interact with other human beings, what Simon referred to as the "artificial world."[5] For each of these contexts, we develop mental models that contribute to our worldview. While it outside the scope of this book to analyze, and explore, all aspects of our worldview, we will instead select some of the most important ones that shape the way we perceive and think, especially in organizational contexts. The book is broken up into several sections (see Table 2.2).

Table 2.2 Mental models addressed in this book

Ref	Book chapters	Aspects of worldview expanded	Mental models developed
I	Cultivate Your Improvisational Capacity	Broadens your view of improvisation and creative expression	Improvisation, decision making
D	Develop Your Design Proficiency	Broadens your view of design and creativity	Design, aesthetics, prototyping
E	Expand your Experimental and Scientific Mind	Broadens your view of the natural world, scientific thinkers, and experimentation	Scientific discovery, learning, experimentation, time and space, causality
A	Deepen Your Aesthetic Awareness	Broadens your view of creative expression and the role of the observer	Aesthetics, beauty, form
S	Capitalize on Your Strengths	Broadens your view of human strengths and intelligence	Intelligence, expertise, creators, learning

In this book, we examine a series of mental models that relate to you as individual. The first area of development pertains to improvisation. Why do people improvise and what is the utility of doing so? How can one become a better improviser? How does improvisation relate to business?

The second area of development pertains to design. What is role of design in life and in business? What makes for good design? What are the characteristics of designers?

In the next chapter, we explore the methods of science and the role of experimentation. In the process we encounter alternative models of reality that challenge the way we think about time, space, causality, and decision making. We also explore the views of the scientists that represent different schools of thought.

The next area for development is aesthetic awareness. How do we perceive and judge the world around us and using what criteria? What is beauty? How does aesthetic awareness relate to everyday life and to the workplace? What criteria do we use to evaluate art or for that matter, products, and services?

The last model we examine is the notion of intelligence. Who is intelligent? How are they intelligent? What emerges is an expanded idea of the many facets of intelligence, and how one can exercise creativity in one or more areas of strength.

For those interested in how mental models shape the performance of teams and organizations, I refer the reader to *Designing Creative High Power Teams and Organizations: Beyond Leadership*, which is also available through Business Expert Press. In the latter, we look at the mental models that have shaped the design of teams and organizations. We look at the power of roles and the characteristics of creators, leaders, managers, and knowledge workers. We look at how to design high performance teams. Also in the same book, we look at models of organizations (e.g., how they are structured and function) and the views regarding employees. Finally, we look at methods of organizational transformation, all of which are based on certain core assumptions.

Mental Models and Assumptions That Hold Us Back

We have met the enemy and he is us.
—Pogo (Walt Kelly)

This book is about ways of seeing and framing the world as much as it is about creativity and design. You cannot really create until you know what you stand for and what your implicit assumptions are about the world. You also will be impeded in your creative development if you are saddled with beliefs and behaviors that are fundamentally limiting. We will look at four main beliefs and behaviors that can impede creative development:

- Language
- Us–them thinking
- Dichotomies
- The voice of judgment

The Power of Language

Language and words shape our reality. Once a thing is assigned a word, it loses its infinite potential and becomes "something." This may seem obvious but it is a little more subtle than that. Consider the following example. Suppose I handed you a plastic bottle filled with water and asked: "Opportunity or problem?" A person selling beverages might say it is an opportunity to quench thirst. On the other hand, an environmentalist might suggest that it is a landfill problem. Of course they are both right. Still another person who is an entrepreneur might see it an opportunity to create a business around recycling. The point is that all things can be labeled problems or opportunities. The hazard of identifying everything as a problem is that it may lead to nonaction, pessimism, rigid thinking, and apathy. The question is: would you rather pursue opportunities or manage problems?

Consider the impact of the following negative statements:

- "I am not creative"
- "I can't draw"
- "I have no talent"
- "I can't change the world"
- "I will never be a leader"

These statements have the immediate effect of stopping you from taking action and making progress toward a goal. In the context of creative thinking, they are idea and action killers. Other more subtle uses of language can impede creative development as well. Consider the following universal statements:

- "The organization will never change."
- "The universe is predictable and governed by laws."
- "We always need a plan."
- "I am only good at one thing."
- "Art has nothing to do with business."
- "Experimentation is the province of science not business."

These types of statements also undermine personal development, especially as it relates to creativity and innovation. Language gives you the power to frame reality in innumerable ways. Be aware of what you might be saying or doing to sabotage your creative efforts.

Us Versus Them Thinking

Another creative trap is employing Us–Them thinking. Here are some examples:

- "She is an artist but I'm not."
- "That's up to the creative people."
- "The leaders in Washington are the problem."

When we use language this way, we immediately play the role of victim, which can lead to passive acceptance of what is. We position ourselves as helpless and at the whim of ever-powerful outside interests. Creators and innovators do not think this way. They do not blame others for problems. In terms of behavioral theory, they maintain an *internal locus of control*. Julian Rotter developed a theory of personality in the 1950s to explain why some people believe they can control their life (and the lives of others), whereas those with an *external locus of control* perceive their lives governed by factors in the environment that they cannot control or influence. Considerable behavioral research has demonstrated that people with an internal locus of control experience higher levels of satisfaction in life and are more successful at work. Designers by definition, as well as other creative people, look to bring things into the world that do not currently exist. They believe that they can mold and shape reality and thus exhibit an internal locus of control. Thinking in terms of Us versus Them simply erodes self-efficacy and empowerment. If you find yourself slipping into this type of thinking, stop, and explore the alternatives. You are indeed the enemy of your own creative thoughts when you think this way.

Dichotomies

Dichotomies are about splitting wholes into distinct parts that are non-overlapping and oftentimes opposites. For example, if we interested in human action, we can divide the world into leaders and followers. The problem with this type of thinking is that it encases us in one category or another. Dichotomies tend to be interpreted in absolute versus existential ways; that is, as rigid for all time versus contingent upon circumstance. The fact is that we are *both* leaders and followers depending on the context. We construct all sorts of dichotomies that limit our potential or the potential of other people. Consider the following:

- Leader–follower
- Initiator–responder
- Active–passive
- Self-actualized–neurotic
- Artist–worker
- Creator–consumer
- Improviser–plodder
- Smart–dumb

When I meet for first time with my graduate students taking a class on creativity in personal and professional life, I usually ask them how many of them consider themselves to be creative. About one-third of the hands go up. I am always surprised because I know that the other two-thirds are much more creative than they give themselves credit for. The latter tend to view "creators" as one of those categories of which they are not a member. As the class progresses and I help them to explore their creative side, at least 50% of those who did not raise their hand have an "Aha!" moment of "I really am creative!" It makes me smile. They have broken down a wall between themselves and this seemingly impenetrable category of being creative. They start to see the world in wholes rather than as fragments of the whole. Seeing the whole is another critical skill for the 21st-century professional.[6] Bottom line: Forget dichotomies.

The Voice of Judgment

There are four primary types of ways that we judge ourselves and others:[7]

- Self-Judgment
- Judgment from others
- Collective judgment
- Judging the judgment

Self-Judgment

This pertains to how we view ourselves and the messages that we send ourselves. We ask ourselves questions like, "Am I successful? Why not?" "Have I been a good daughter or son? Why not?" In a more harsh way, we might say things like, "You are just an old fool," or "Why do I do always do things to mess up my life?" It is OK to reflect but not to self-castigate. Most of the time, these musings are the product of things left over from childhood; that is, unresolved issues with parents or siblings, relationships with peers, or coming to terms with codes of conduct. These types of judgments seriously impede creative expression because they undermine a sense of self and core identity. Taking the creative plunge is difficult enough when outside critics abound. My advice is to take the self-critic out of the mix. Plenty of people will give you feedback, both positive and negative, along the way.

Judgment From Others

This is an inevitable part of the creative journey. It is not uncommon for successful artists, designers, and musicians to confess later in life that one or more teachers or mentors told them they had "no talent." Let me give you an example.

My father chose music as his life's profession, specifically playing jazz piano. His first music teacher (he started on saxophone) told him to give up the instrument because he would "never amount to anything." Later, his first piano teacher told him he "had no talent." He came from a modest background in Philadelphia, and his father was a butcher. His family did not understand him or jazz music, or why he would stay out late at night "jamming." They called him a "bum." Fortunately, he didn't listen to them. He practiced many hours a day both classical and jazz music. He later took lessons with Gregory Ashman, the piano accompanist to the great violinist Efrem Zimbalist. My father became a superb and nationally recognized pianist and played with the likes of Charlie Parker and Dizzy Gillespie. He wrote several books on piano, recorded numerous historic jazz recordings, and even played for President Jimmy Carter. Who was included in the band at the White House? Louie Armstrong! The picture hangs in my office. The point is: take what others say about you with a grain of salt. It may be true that your craft needs work at a certain point. However, it should not deter from your goals and dreams. Don't internalize or "agree" with these assessments. Listen, learn, and move on.

Collective Judgment

This form of judgment refers to the values and norms imposed by the culture we are born into. Values and norms are socially constructed and change overtime. Certain things considered acceptable in one decade may not be the next such as the length of clothes, the shape of our bodies, what we are allowed to say (or not say) for fear of ridicule or scorn. It can also pertain to the values and norms (i.e., culture) of the organization you work for. Are people expected to stay after 5 pm? Work well in teams? Manage work–life balance in favor of the company? The culture of an organization, as well as society, can play a huge role in fostering or impeding your creativity. Organizations such as Google that embrace creative thinking may align incentives with personal development by offering employees paid time to "think," "doodle," or work on "dream" projects. Most of us are less fortunate and have to contend with the opposite. The key is to remember that all great designers and creative people had to contend with, and adapt to, the mores of the times they were born into. To paraphrase a saying familiar among entrepreneurs, "You are not really trying until you tick someone off."[8] Don't be afraid to cross disciplinary and cultural boundaries. You may be setting a future trend.

Judging the Judgment

This form of judgment is also detrimental to creative development. It pertains to ruminations about the efficacy of the first three types of judgment. "Was he right about my lack of talent?" "My work really is bad; I might as well give up," "Normal people would not spend time doing this." Again, it takes discipline to stop these destructive ruminations. Don't build an internal feedback loop that amplifies the magnitude of the judgments from other sources. Keep these thoughts in perspective and focus on what you can do now to either improve or change course. You have degrees of freedom.

Counteracting Negative Thinking

There are several things you can do to mitigate the negative effects of judgment and negative thinking. Here are three that are effective:[9]

- Pay attention to your thoughts.
- Attack the judgment.
- Make the judgment look ridiculous.

Whenever you find yourself slipping into any of the types of judgments or negative thought patterns noted earlier, do the following. First, take note of your thoughts. Awareness is the first step to making change. A useful practice is to write down negative thoughts as they occur. Divide a sheet of paper into two columns. On the left, write down your negative thoughts. In the right-hand column attack the judgment by refuting it or making it look ridiculous. Logically and systematically you should be able to downgrade the efficacy of each negative thought or barrier. There are many examples of ideas and inventions that were derided that later transformed the world. Airplanes. The phonograph. Space flight. Personal computers. Flash drives. Use these examples to diminish and make fun of the naysayers of the world.

Promote the Beginner's Mind

Once you have cleared away the impediments to creative thought, you need to cultivate practices that enhance your ability to create. Cultivating curiosity[10] is critical; that is, to embrace your curiosity about the world that you had as a child. Watch children play. They simply act for the sheer delight of it. They are not saddled with the judgments and negative thoughts that emerge as we mature into adults. They simply are who they are in that instant. This is the attitude that each of us has to cultivate to maximize our creative potential. Zen practitioners refer to this characteristic as *cultivating the beginner's mind*. Suzuki[11] writes, "In the beginner's mind there are many possibilities, but in the expert's there are few."

When I teach a course on creativity to MBAs, I have my students learn about themselves by taking pictures of everyday objects with a camera. For that 30-minute period, these serious working professionals scamper around the building taking pictures as if they were children. I hear them laugh or see them sprawled out on the floor (sometimes in work clothes!) attempting to get the perfect picture of a yellow ball I gave them which is their subject. The slide shows they put together are impressive, and even they are amazed at their own creativity and the creativity of others. While some of them are new to the world of photography and truly are beginners, but many are not. One student, a seasoned photographer, blurted out, "I usually focus on the technical aspects of what I shoot. Today, armed only with a cell phone camera, I didn't but instead really looked at my subjects and composition. I really saw. What a great change!" In that instant, he was no longer an expert, but a beginner seeing the world for the first time filled with possibility.

Exercises such as these help us to cultivate awareness, mindfulness, and the faculties of perception, which are all essential for creative expression. Another useful practice is meditation. Meditation comes in many forms but simply means to reserve a short period of time each day to quiet your mind or let it "drift." It is not about problem solving or sleeping. It is a space to let thoughts emerge and disappear and to focus on the immediacy of your surroundings. In short, it is about being *present*. Being present and immersed in flow is a requirement for creative expression and meditation can help achieve this state. Suzuki's "Zen Mind, Beginner's Mind" is an excellent resource in this regard. Another wonderful book on being present and mindful is, "Zen in the Art of Archery."[12] The author was a professor of philosophy from Germany, who visited Japan. He chronicles his practice of archery as a means to access the foundations of Zen. His short book will change your view of the world and yourself.

Reflective Practice

Here are a few additional exercises that can help you to accelerate the transformation of your mental models.

Reflective Practice 2.1: Find a partner and discuss a new product or service your company is launching or you are thinking of bringing to market. Assume you are colleagues. One person should invite the other person to support the project. The responder should begin each sentence with the word, "No, ..." Do this for about 3–4 minutes and then switch roles. At the completion of the exercise, discuss the experience. How did it go? What did it feel like? How did the word "no" help or hinder your progress? What other word could you use to respond with at the start of the sentence?[13]

Reflective Practice 2.2: Think about the negative effects of Us versus Them thinking in the workplace. Oftentimes sales complains about manufacturing, marketing pits itself versus finance, or stockholders are viewed as the bane of management. What are the negative consequences of this type of thinking? Who are the "others" in your workplace or social context?

Reflective Practice 2.3: Identify 10 dichotomies that you use. What are the negative consequences of this at work? What are the negative consequences for your career or for your personal development?

Chapter Summary

Mental models, assumptions, and language exert a powerful influence on our capacity for creative thinking and design. All your mental models taken together compose your worldview. While it is unrealistic to change your complete worldview overnight, you can change one or more of your mental models and core assumptions over time. Furthermore, you can pay close attention to the words that you use and the conceptual frameworks you employ. Look for opportunities rather than be taken down by problems. Avoid characterizing the environment as an unchanging enemy. Think in terms of wholes rather than to use dichotomies. Temper the voice of judgment of yourself and others. Most importantly, foster your child-like wonder of the world. Really pay attention to your surroundings by being present and mindful. All of these changes will reformat you to reach your creative potential.

CHAPTER 3

Capitalize on Your Strengths

It's not that I'm so smart, it's just that I stay with problems longer.
—Albert Einstein, scientist

Often the hands will solve a mystery that the intellect has struggled with in vain.

—Carl Jung, psychologist

Numerous studies have shown that expertise and creativity emerge in relation to a particular domain of knowledge or activity. For example, we might say that a particular person is gifted as an artist, a musician, a writer, or leader. Human beings exhibit an astonishing array of strengths and abilities. To become really good or even "gifted" requires that we spend considerable time developing our innate talents, strengths, and abilities. Therefore, one of the first steps in our journey is to assess our cognitive, kinesthetic, and perceptual abilities using the tools that have been designed for such measurement. Historically, human beings were assessed in terms of their *general* cognitive abilities using IQ scores. While a start, studies have shown that such measures are inadequate predictors of creative ability, potential or otherwise. On the other hand, a much more pragmatic and useful approach is to use the theory of Multiple Intelligences as a guide to creative development. We will discuss each in turn.

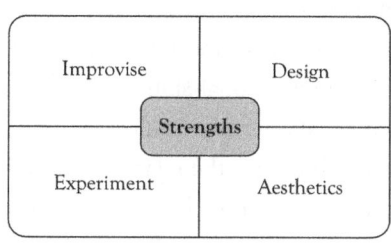

Standard Measures of Intelligence

One of the first psychometric measures developed to gauge a person's intellectual horsepower was the standard Intelligence Quotient (IQ) test. This test has a long and contentious history. Motivation to classify humans according to intellectual factors began as early as the mid-1880s largely through the work of Francis Galton, who spearheaded the eugenics movement. Eugenics was an attempt to improve the human species through selective breeding. Although eugenics was soundly rejected and discredited, the search for measures to differentiate between human beings in terms of their intellectual capabilities carried on.

By the early part of the 20th century, Alfred Binet and Théodore Simon, two French psychologists, devised a more refined and rigorous test to measure IQ. Binet believed that intelligence could change over a person's lifetime and was influenced by environmental factors. His motivation for developing the test was to identify children with special needs so that they could be provided with assistance. The standard IQ scale distributes human beings along a continuum with 120 considered "average." By the 1940s, David Wechsler reformulated the scoring system. The general intelligence score (g) is the one most widely used today.

The relationship between general intelligence scores and other outcomes in life has been studied extensively and the results are mixed at best. Despite early claims[1] that intelligence is a good predictor of many factors including financial income, job performance, pregnancy, or crime (and better than family socioeconomic status or education level), subsequent studies have found limited support for these hypotheses.

The American Psychological Association's established a task force to examine the relationship between IQ and other measures and outcomes in life. The report[2] found that "intelligence test scores are at least weakly related to job performance in most settings ... such tests predict considerably less than half the variance of job-related measures. Other individual characteristics such as interpersonal skills, aspects of personality, and so forth are probably of equal or greater importance."[3]

Another important finding is the relationship between IQ scores and specific subjects studied in school that can lead to certain professions. One study[4] found that correlations between g and achievement ranged from 58.6% in mathematics to 48% in English. On the other hand, g was only correlated 18.1% with art and design. This is significant. If we look carefully at Table 3.1, the implications are obvious, as well as statistically significant.

The results indicate that there is considerable variance between general intelligence and achievement in each subject. While g is somewhat of a predictor of achievement in subjects such as mathematics and English,[5] it is by no means assured. In another study,[6] the correlation between g and SAT scores[7] was 0.82, but in another set of measurements it was only 0.4.[8] High levels of variance within a study *measuring the same thing* or between instruments supposedly measuring the same thing is never a good outcome.

Furthermore, Table 3.1 indicates that g is a relatively poor predictor of creative endeavors such as art and design (0.18), music (.0.28), and graphics (0.21). All correlations here are below 0.3. It is also a poor predictor of excellence in information technology skills, business, sports, and even the hard sciences, such as physics and chemistry. Again, all correlations are below 0.34. Thus, *general IQ cannot be used to predict future success in many professions*. At best, IQ is only useful at predicting success in narrow domains of knowledge such as English and mathematics. This information can only be used in *conjunction* with evidence of other skills and abilities to identify the potential for professional success.

From a pragmatic view, IQ gives the recipient no clear idea of his or her cognitive, perceptual, or kinesthetic strengths, either current or potential. General intelligence is thus a very limited measure for our purposes and does not serve to identify specific areas of strength nor does it predict areas for development. What we need is a measure that identifies areas of strength that we currently possess and ones that can target for development. The Theory of Multiple Intelligences is designed to do just that.

Theory of Multiple Intelligences

Howard Gardner,[9] a noted educational theorist from Harvard University, proposed a different approach to the standard IQ. He argued that we need to measure a wider range of what he referred to as intelligences (also

Table 3.1 *Correlations between IQ scores (CAT g) and achievement in specific subjects*

Subject	CAT g	N
Arts and Humanities		
English	0.483	67,677
English literature	0.383	62,416
Drama	**0.226**	10,997
Religious Education	0.303	13,572
French	0.448	36,370
German	0.402	16,638
Spanish	0.413	6501
Science		
Mathematics	0.589	68,125
Double Science	0.465	59,518
Single Science	0.361	5331
Physics	**0.244**	2733
Chemistry	**0.215**	2720
Biology	**0.264**	2764
Social Sciences		
Geography	0.443	26,081
History	0.406	22,764
Business	**0.336**	11,188
Information Technology	**0.228**	9350
Information Technology (short class)	**0.234**	8931
Practical		
Art and Design	**0.182**	15,104
Music	**0.288**	5208
Physical Education	**0.303**	13,846
DT-Food	**0.294**	13,493
DT-Graphics	**0.211**	14,328
DT-Resistant Materials	**0.223**	14,059
DT-Textiles	**0.263**	6390

Notes: General Certificate of Secondary Education (GCSE) examinations are offered in a wide range of subjects and are graded from A to G. For the purposes of the analyses, these were scored from 8 to 0, respectively. Values shown are η^2 for each fixed effect and covariate in the model. Correlations under 0.34 are shown in bold.

Source: Deary et al. (2007, 18). Only most relevant parts of table provided.

Table 3.2 Areas of multiple intelligence

Area	Description
Verbal–linguistic intelligence	Well-developed verbal skills and sensitivity to the sounds, meanings, and rhythms of words
Mathematical–logical intelligence	Ability to think conceptually and abstractly, and capacity to discern logical or numerical patterns
Musical intelligence	Ability to produce and appreciate rhythm, pitch, and timber
Visual–spatial intelligence	Capacity to think in images and pictures, to visualize accurately and abstractly
Bodily kinesthetic intelligence	Ability to control one's body movements and to handle objects skillfully
Interpersonal intelligence	Capacity to detect and respond appropriately to the moods, motivations, and desires of others
Intrapersonal intelligence	Capacity to be self-aware and in tune with inner feelings, values, beliefs, and thinking processes
Naturalist intelligence	Ability to recognize and categorize plants, animals, and other objects in nature

referred to as strengths). The standard IQ and other tests such as the SAT focus on verbal and mathematical or logical abilities. Although these are useful, he argues after observing hundreds and hundreds of children and adults that we have a broader range of intelligences. These include the eight intelligences shown in Table 3.2.

He also speculated that there is also a "half-intelligence" which he calls "existential intelligence." Existential intelligence is defined as having a sensitivity and capacity to tackle deep questions about human existence, such as the meaning of life, why do we die, and how we got here.

These intelligences are not given at birth but can be molded and shaped throughout a person's lifetime. Gardner examines some of the more notable examples of people who have risen to the top in each of these categories. These include the people shown in Table 3.3.

He argues that each of these individuals attained exceptionally high levels of performance because they may have had innate talents in certain areas as children, *and* they worked very hard for several years to attain mastery.[10]

Table 3.3 Multiple intelligence exemplars[11]

Verbal–Linguistic Intelligence	Mathematical–Logical Intelligence	Musical Intelligence
Virginia Wolfe	Albert Einstein	Mozart
Visual–Spatial Intelligence	Bodily–Kinesthetic Intelligence	Interpersonal Intelligence
Picasso	Martha Graham	Margaret Thatcher
Intrapersonal Intelligence	Naturalist Intelligence	Existential Intelligence[12]
Ghandi	Charles Darwin	Rene Descartes

Herbert Simon's work on expertise confirms that people need to accumulate at least 50,000 "chunks" of learning episodes to really master a domain.[13] This is on the order of 5 to 10 years. Gardner also observes that the average interval of time between major creative works is about 10 years.[14] Malcolm Gladwell[15] also suggests that 10,000 hours is the period of time required to reach critical mass in terms of expertise and insight. Figure 3.1 illustrates the relationship between practice, mastery, and creative skill level.

The main point is that hard work, not just natural abilities or high IQ, often determine a person's ultimate success and level of expertise in a particular métier or domain. This is good news for the rest of us. If we work really hard with the appropriate educational guidance, then we can attain

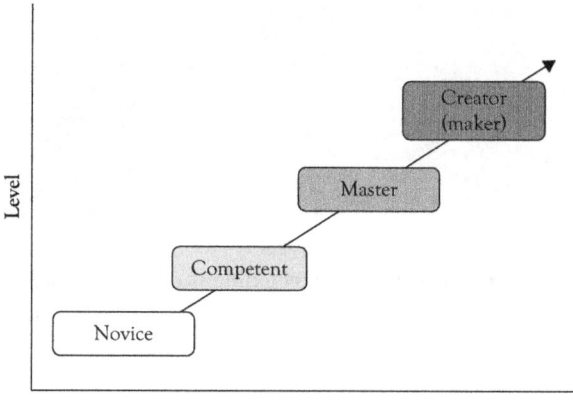

Time >>

Figure 3.1 Relationship between development time and skill attainment[16]

significant levels of mastery in a particular craft. The real question is: where do we start? To answer that question, you first need to assess where you are today. You may do this by using a tool to assess your multiple intelligences. My suggestion before reading further is to execute a Google search for "multiple intelligence assessment" to find the most up-to-date links.[17] Once you have taken the assessment, please read on.

Interpreting Your Multiple Intelligence Profile

The interesting thing about your profile is that it represents two things: *areas of strength* and *areas for development*. How strong you are in a particular intelligence is a measure of your abilities and *how much time you have spent in that domain of knowledge*. You either have spent time developing an area because you or someone else thought it was a good idea. If you picked it, then it is likely to be correlated with a measure of satisfaction. Even training for a few hours can result in significant changes in the quality of the output as illustrated in Figure 3.2.

If someone else picked the area (e.g., parents, mentors, friends, boss), then you may or may not find the activities in that area to be satisfying. *It is up to you to decide where to put your time and energy*. On the flip side, the areas in which you score low not only may be a reflection of your abilities

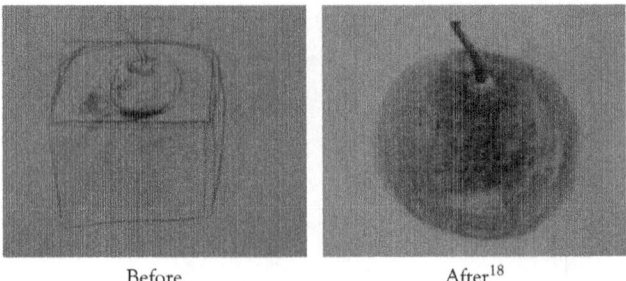

Before   After[18]

Figure 3.2 Impact of technical development on artistic achievement[19]

but also may be a reflection of where you have chosen to spend your time. It is unreasonable to assume that you would be good at something that you have spent little time in. For example, you can't expect yourself to draw realistic trees or people if the only experience you had occurred in the third grade. However, your level of proficiency can be developed at any time. It is up to you to decide where and when to apply yourself to a particular area.

Multiple Intelligence Composite Scores

In addition to the top and bottom scores on your multiple intelligence profile, it is important to look at the combinations of strengths that you possess. The top two or more strengths create composites that map to other macro qualities such as jobs or professions.

For example, in Table 3.4, we look at pairings of verbal–linguistic intelligence with each of the other intelligences on the list. These pairings produce seven 2D composites. Famous people who represent these combinations are identified as well.

For example, Brian Greene is a good example of someone who combines verbal–linguistic intelligence with mathematical–logical intelligence. Brian, a physicist, is best known for narrating the popular PBS series "The Elegant Universe," which examines the history of modern physics and the emergence of string theory. Tim McCarver, like other athletes who make the transition to television, represents a combination of kinesthetic intelligence and verbal–linguistic intelligence. All

Table 3.4 *Examples of multiple intelligence 2D composites*

MI-1	MI-2	Example	Discipline
Mathematical–logical intelligence	Verbal–linguistic intelligence	Brian Green	Astrophysicist/PBS narrator
Musical intelligence	Verbal–linguistic intelligence	Bono	U2-band/spokesperson
Visual–spatial intelligence	Verbal–linguistic intelligence	Jimmy Carter	Engineering/politics
Bodily kinesthetic intelligence	Verbal–linguistic intelligence	Tim McCarver	Baseball/announcer
Interpersonal intelligence	Verbal–linguistic intelligence	Barack Obama	Community organizer/politics
Intrapersonal intelligence	Verbal–linguistic intelligence	Dr. Phil	Psychology/talk show
Naturalist intelligence	Verbal–linguistic intelligence	Jacques Cousteau	Oceanography/television

in all, there are twenty-eight composite 2D combinations.[20] A matrix of all 2D combinations that includes examples of people who closely resemble each of these strength pairings (as well as related professions) is provided at the end of the chapter in Table 3.5. These examples are instructive because they suggest opportunities for personal development. Few of us will attain the stature of a Mozart or a Picasso. More likely, we will develop two or more strengths to a lesser degree but that does not mean we are destined to obscurity. Developing two or more areas of strength can position us to become high-level achievers and creators in a wide variety of existing and emerging domains. For example, novel web technologies have opened up new media niches not imagined 10 years ago and those with requisite strengths are finding opportunities using blogs, online video, and tweets. So, our challenge is to identify and commit to the development of those areas of strength that fit these new economic niches and that give us the most overall satisfaction. Furthermore, it is in these deep pools of expertise that creative ideas manifest themselves. To be creative requires us to really master a domain, which is why we need to get started on the road as quickly as possible. Investing 10,000 hours takes considerable effort, but the results are worth it.

Table 3.5 Examples of combinations of multiple intelligences

	Linguistic	Math/Logical	Visual/Spatial	Bodily/Kinesthetic	Musical	Interpersonal	Intrapersonal	Naturalist
Linguistic	Attorney, journalist, poet, public relations director. Examples: Virginia Wolfe	Science educator/scholar	Comic book artist, graphic artist, advertising agent	Sportscaster	Opera/music theater composer, music lyricist, rapper	Translator, motivational speaker, comedian, historian	Writer: humanist, transcendentalist	Tour guide, nature show host, natural historian
Math/Logical	Carl Sagan (TV host, cosmologist), Bill Nye (TV host of "Bill Nye the Science Guy"), Brian Greene (physicist)	Accountant, Computer repair, Electrical engineer, Scientist. Examples: Albert Einstein	Videographer/Cameraman, Cinematographer, Film Director	Robotics engineer, mechanical engineer, physician	Audio engineer, music technician	Financial guru, operations manager	Technology innovator	Cartographer, environmental engineer, cosmologist
Visual/Spatial	Stan Lee (comic book author, Marvel Comics), Dr. Seuss (children's book author/illustrator)	Stephen Spielberg (film director, "Jaws"), George Lucas (film director, "Star Wars"), Stanley Kubrick (film director, "2001: A Space Odyssey"), Alfred Hitchcock (suspense film director and TV producer/host)	Architect, Pilot, Interior Designer, Artist. Examples: Pablo Picasso	Choreographer, Puppeteer, Animator	Set designer, music video director/producer, mixed media performer	Film producer, museum curator, marketing manager	Magician	Wildlife photographer/painter
Bodily/Kinesthetic	Howie Long (sportscaster, former NFL defensive end), Terry Bradshaw (sportscaster, former NFL quarterback), John Madden (sportscaster, former NFL head coach)	Robert Zemekis (film director known for special effects and motion capture), Cynthia Breazeal (director of Personal Robots Group at MIT Labs)	Paula Abdul (choreographer, former pop star), Jim Henson (puppeteer, creator of "The Muppets"), Walt Disney (animator, creator of Mickey Mouse)	Athlete, Dancer, Actor. Examples: Martha Graham	Musical theatre performer	Fitness instructor, trainer, massage therapist	Martial artist, yoga instructor	Dietician, rock climber, animal trainer, ski instructor

(Continued)

	Linguistic	Math/Logical	Visual/Spatial	Bodily/Kinesthetic	Musical	Interpersonal	Intrapersonal	Naturalist
Musical	George and Ira Gershwin (composer/lyricist team), Alan Menken, & Howard Ashman (composer/lyricist team), Stephen Sondheim (composer and lyricist, "Sweeney Todd"), George Bizet (opera composer, "Carmen"), Andrew Lloyd Webber (music theatre composer, "Evita"), Dr. Dre (rapper, music producer)	Leo Fender (inventor of Fender guitar amps), George Martin (sound engineer for The Beatles), Bob Ludwig (mastering engineer for many music legends)	Blue Man Group (electronic music and performance group), Daft Punk (electronic music group), Gorillaz (mixed media rock group), Michael Jackson (pop star, dancer)	Jason Alexander (actor), Bernadette Peters (Broadway actress), Cast of Stomp! (Broadway dance show)	**Choir Director, Music Teacher, Songwriter, Vocalist. Examples: Wolfgang A. Mozart, Igor Stravinsky**	Music therapist, music educator, pedagogy/technique developer	Music record mogul, music/entertainment producer	Sound designer, foley artist, luthier
Interpersonal	Tony Robbins (motivational speaker)	Henry Ford (industrialist, Model-T developer), Jim Cramer (finance TV personality), Suze Orman (TV financial advisor), David Ramsey (financial author)	Mark Burnett (TV producer, "Survivor" and "The Apprentice"), Brad Bird (Pixar film director, "The Incredibles")	Charles Atlas (bodybuilder), Jack LaLanne (fitness expert), Denise Austin (fitness instructor)	Zoltan Kodaly (music theory teacher, Kodaly method), Shinichi Suzuki (teacher/developer of Suzuki method), Nadia Boulanger (legendary music composition instructor)	**Manager, Politician, Counselor, Nurse, Salesperson, Teacher. Example: Gandhi**	CEO, team-building consultant	Zoologist, environmentalist, activist
Intrapersonal	Walt Whitman (author, "Leaves of Grass")	Steve Jobs (CEO and co-founder of Apple), Bill Gates (philanthropist, co-founder and former CEO of Microsoft)	Harry Houdini (magician, escapologist), David Copperfield (illusionist), David Blaine (illusionist)	Bruce Lee (actor, martial art instructor)	Quincy Jones (musician, TV and music producer), Miles Davis (trumpeter, jazz composer)	Dale Carnegie (writer and self-improvement lecturer), Warren Buffett (investor, CEO of Berkshire Hathaway)	**Writers, Clergy, Entrepreneur, Psychologist. Example: Dr. Sigmund Freud, Howard Gardner**	Zen monk
Naturalist	Steve Irwin (TV nature show host), Jack Hanna (zookeeper), Henry David Thoreau (naturalist, author of "Walden")	Stephen Hawking (cosmologist)	John James Audubon (ornithologist, painter), Ansel Adams (photographer, environmentalist)	Dr. Robert Atkins (physician, developer of Atkins Diet), Sir Edmund Hillary (mountaineer, reached summit of Mount Everest)	Stradivarius (luthier), John Cage (composer, percussionist)	Al Gore (environmentalist, lecturer, former V.P. of U.S.A)	Frank Gehry (architect, Guggenheim Bilbao, Spain)	**Biologist, Farmer, Meteorologist, Veterinarian. Example: Charles Darwin**

Chapter Summary

Each person has certain abilities and strengths. For some people, it is an ability to communicate with others. Others are good at mathematics, sports, or even thinking. The point is that each of us has a distinct composite of strengths upon which to build a foundation for creative development. In order to express new and novel ideas in a particular domain requires time and hard work. We must master our chosen domain in order to create within it. Our biggest is challenge is to *choose* and *commit* to a particular path for development. It will take years (as many as 10 years) to produce extraordinary work. The key is to get started now.

CHAPTER 4

Cultivate Your Improvisational Capacity

Improvisation is too good to leave to chance.
—Paul Simon, musician

The genius of our country is improvisation, and jazz reflects that. It's our great contribution to the arts.

—Ken Burns, author

If it's a modern-day story dealing with certain ethnic groups, I think I could open up certain scenes for improvisation, while staying within the structure of the script.

—Martin Scorsese, filmmaker

What do you do when there is no plan or the plan makes no sense given the conditions? You improvise. Consider this event:

The pilots of U.S. Airways Flight 1549 achieved one of the rarest and most technically challenging feats in commercial aviation: landing on water without fatalities.

Although commercial jetliners are equipped with life vests and inflatable slides, there have been few successful attempts at water landings during the jet age. Indeed, even though pilots go through the motions of learning to ditch a plane in water, the generally held belief is that such landings would almost certainly result in fatalities.

Capt. Chesley B. Sullenberger III, a veteran U.S. Airways pilot, pulled it off while simultaneously coping with numerous other challenges.[1]

Was this a stroke of luck? Fate? Skill? I would argue that Captain Sullenberger was a successful improviser because he was so well trained in standard routines. Huh? What does training have to do with improvisation? As it turns out, everything.

Improvisation is the least understood new skill to gain personal competitive advantage. Let's take a deep dive into what it means to improvise and to explode some of the misperceptions concerning it. We begin by defining improvisation and follow by scoping out the contexts most likely to require improvisation. Captain Sullenberger performed in what is considered a high-risk/low-structure *real-time decision-making* context. Real time in this case is defined as decisions that must be made within seconds or minutes. Improvisation is sometimes the only response to a real-time decision-making context. Let's explore these concepts.

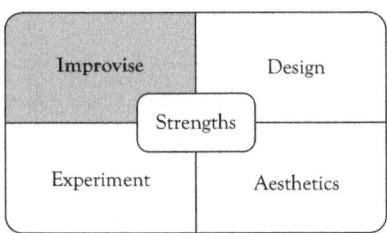

Defining Improvisation

Common-use definitions of improvisation[2] include the following characteristics:

- To invent, compose, or perform something extemporaneously.
- To improvise music.
- To make do with whatever materials are at hand.

The roots of the word come from the Latin derivative *proviso,* which means to stipulate beforehand or to foresee. The prefix *im* means not; that is, the negation of what follows. Hence, the word *improvisation* can be interpreted to mean *unforeseen* or to take action in the moment. That being said, the concept of improvisation is far more nuanced and rich than these simple definitions suggest. Improvisation does not simply arise out of nowhere; that is, it is grounded in prior work in a particular discipline. Consider the following definition in the context of jazz music:

> Improvisation involves reworking pre-composed material and designs in relation to unanticipated ideas conceived shaped and transformed under the special conditions of performance, thereby adding unique features to every creation.[3]

Put another way: "Improvisation involves exploring, continual experimenting, tinkering with possibilities without knowing where one's queries will lead or how action will unfold."[4] Furthermore, the sometimes mistaken notion that during improvisation, the decision maker simply makes things up in the moment without rigor or structure is inaccurate and many would argue that nothing could be further from the truth:

> The popular definitions of improvisation that emphasize only its spontaneous, intuitive nature ... are astonishingly incomplete. This simplistic understanding belies the discipline and experience on which improvisers depend, and it obscures the actual practices and processes that engage them. Improvisation depends ... on thinkers having absorbed a broad base of ... knowledge, including myriad conventions that contribute to formulating ideas logically, cogently, and expressively.[5]

In order to be able to respond effectively in context, the improviser must have at his or her disposal sets of routines and packets of knowledge that roughly match that context. In other words, you "can't improvise on nothing; you got to improvise on something."[6] The improviser must modify the routines to fit the novel conditions that exist for a given situation.

Making effective decisions in real-time group contexts requires that the decision maker make sense of what is being communicated by others in the moment and to self-reflect (or hear) the words and behaviors uttered by him or herself. Weick[7] refers to this as *retrospective sense-making*. The latter requires the ability to self-monitor and listen to one's own voice. It also requires extensive memory to assess resources and make choices. "If you are not affected and influenced by your own notes [or ideas] when you improvise then you're missing the whole point."[8]

Finally, improvisation is *process-oriented* as opposed to *output-oriented.* This distinction is made clear by comparing improvisation to innovation. Although Peter Drucker[9] defined innovation as change that results in new levels of performance, he is referring to the outputs of such change (e.g., the creation of goods or services) rather than to the performance itself. Put another way: "Innovation is the embodiment, combination, or synthesis of knowledge in original, relevant, valued new products, processes, or services."[10] Improvisation on the other hand focuses on the *quality of the performance* as opposed to the artifacts that may result from such activity.

Here is the working definition of improvisation that we shall use in this book:

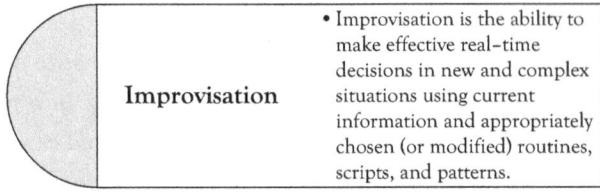

Improvisation

• Improvisation is the ability to make effective real-time decisions in new and complex situations using current information and appropriately chosen (or modified) routines, scripts, and patterns.

Examples of Improvisers

Improvisers are real-time designers. They design through performance and action. For example, a jazz musician will craft a solo from start to finish based on a certain "vocabulary" of "words," in this case, cascades of sound and rhythm. Similarly, entrepreneurs improvise products, services, and processes, especially in the start-up phase when resources may be scarce. Great improvisers appear in all fields and a few are shown in Table 4.1.

Miles Davis is one of my favorite jazz artists and composers. Born in 1926, the son of a wealthy dentist, Miles grew up in St. Louis and studied music at the age of 13. He was admitted to the Julliard School of Music in New York City in 1944, but dropped out the next year to play professionally as a jazz musician with Charlie "Bird" Parker, the great alto saxophonist. For the next 10 years he played with a host of jazz greats, drifted in and out of drugs, and made several record albums that were a prelude of things to come. By 1956 he began a series of recordings that

Table 4.1 Examples of great improvisers[11]

Miles Davis[12] (musician-composer)	Sandy Lerner and Len Bosack[13] (Founders of Cisco)	Mark Zuckerberg[14] (Founder of Facebook)
Crew of Apollo 13	Firefighters	Surgical teams

demonstrated his rise as a player and band leader: "Relaxin' with the Miles Davis Quintet," "Steamin' with the Miles Davis Quintet," "Workin' with the Miles Davis Quintet," and "Cookin' with the Miles Davis Quintet." In 1959, he recorded his best and the most popular jazz album of all time (over 4 million sold), titled, "Kind of Blue" featuring Bill Evans (piano), Wynton Kelly (piano), Paul Chambers (bass), John Coltrane (sax), Cannonball Adderley (sax), and Jimmy Cobb (drums). This album so changed the course of jazz music (and music in general) it was voted by Congress to be recognized as a national treasure. It is ranked by Rolling Stone Magazine as No. 12 on the list of the 500 greatest albums of all time. The improvisations are amazing. Listen to it.

Sandy Lerner and Len Bosack (a husband and wife team) started one of the largest companies in the world, Cisco Systems, in their modest home near Stanford University in 1984. What began as an experiment to connect various networks at the university turned into a major enterprise with revenues of over $49 billion in 2013, 70,000 employees and a market valuation of over $120 billion (2013).[15] As improvisers, they constructed the original networks in their living room, bedroom, and kitchen. They financed the company on credit cards prior to receiving venture capital from Sequoia Capital of Menlo Park, California. Improvising the technology and the business model until they became successful was how they left their mark, and the results are impressive. Almost every networking ability available today can be traced back to Cisco Systems.

Mark Zuckerberg at the grand old age of 20 started Facebook in 2004. Since then it has grown to be the largest social networking site in the world, boasting over *one billion* users as of 2013. Zuckerberg and his staff were true designers or improvisers in the sense that they tinkered with the look and feel of the service from the start. They added features such as the News Feed (2006), fan/like pages, poking, status updates, photo albums, messaging, and blogs ("Notes"), which allowed them to retain and grow their client base. Sometimes it is forgotten that MySpace had a commanding lead on Facebook (by tens of millions of users) until April 2008, when Facebook unseated it. They essentially defined the social networking experience. By remaining flexible, nimble, and not afraid to take risks, Facebook has risen to the top aided and abetted by its chief improviser, Mark Zuckerberg.

The Crew of Apollo 13 included Commander James A. Lovell, John L. "Jack" Swigert as Command Module pilot and Fred W. Haise as Lunar Module pilot. Launched on April 11, 1970, the spacecraft sustained a life-threatening explosion 200,000 miles from Earth. The number 2 oxygen tank exploded because of a short circuit and a decision was made to abort the mission to get the crew back to Earth. To accomplish that feat, the crew and Mission Control in Houston, had to improvise a return making use of the limited supplies of power to the engines and the limited air available to the astronauts. The lunar command module was converted into a kind of lifeboat, although it was originally designed for 2 days of life support not the 4 days that were needed to get the crew of three safely back. In what was one of the greatest engineering improvisations of all time, the crew safely returned to Earth on April 17. See the movie. It dramatizes the events convincingly.

I have included two other examples of improvisers above: surgical teams and firefighters. Both teams may be forced to improvise as real-time conditions change. We address these issues later in the chapter as well in the companion book to this one: *Designing Creative High Power Teams and Organizations: Beyond Leadership*, which is also available through Business Expert Press. It should be pointed out that most improvisation takes place *in a context with other people working in teams*.

Table 4.2 Improvisation and design contexts

Context	Sub-area	Design (Composition)	Improvisation
Performing arts	Music	Classical	Jazz
	Theater	Opera	Improvisational theater
	Dance	Ballet	Jazz
	Comedy	Comedy shows	Improvisational comedy
Visual arts		Finished works of art	Doing art studies, sketches
Literary arts		Novels, poems, essays	Telling stories
Engineering		Buildings, products	Building models
Management		New product development; for example, iPod	Responding to crisis; for example, Tylenol; problem solving
Medicine		Routine surgical procedures or protocols	"Unexpected" and complex surgeries
Training[16]		Manuals and workbooks; instructional design	Navigating through simulated worlds such as Second Life and other games

Contexts in Which People Improvise

We see examples of improvisation in many different fields ranging from music to business to medicine. In Table 4.2, I outline several areas of activity aligned with improvisation. We contrast this with *design* or *composition*. The latter are contexts that result in the creation of ideas, activities, and artifacts where there are no short-term time constraints. Design and improvisation are related by output but differentiated by process.

There are many types of improvisational contexts as illustrated earlier. We can differentiate contexts by classifying them according to two important characteristics: (1) the *degree of structure of the problem space* and (2) the *degree of risk* of actions taken, where risk is defined as the likelihood of outcomes that bear consequences for any and all stakeholders. For example, in jazz, a primary stakeholder is the listener. In health care, the primary stakeholder is the patient and his or her family.

Simon[17] defined the degree of structure of the problem space (e.g., structured to unstructured) to evaluate different problem-solving contexts[18] Structure in this case refers to the degree that the problem-solving domain can be conceptualized and that procedures, methods, and decision aids be developed to support the decision maker. For example, frequently performed surgical procedures tend to become structured problem spaces over time as the surgery is refined and standards evolve. On the other hand, introducing a new smartphone or novel technology into the marketplace is considered a low structure context since limited experiential knowledge is available to the decision makers.

The second dimension, outcome risk, is referred to as the *magnitude of consequences* by theorists who study business ethics.[19] Magnitude of consequences captures the notion that actions that result in more severe consequences (e.g., death, dismemberment, etc.) are deemed to have higher moral intensity, all other things being equal. Magnitude of Consequences (MoC) is defined as "...the sum of the harms (or benefits) done to victims (or beneficiaries) of the moral act in question."[20]

Improvisational contexts may be delineated by these two dimensions, thus giving rise to the classification in Table 4.3.

These four quadrants allow us to categorize most improvisational contexts. For example, traditional jazz music is considered a high structure, low-risk context. Traditional jazz (e.g., Dixieland) has a well-defined set of rules and structures that define the music within which the improviser can take liberties. This is contrasted with "free jazz" that minimizes most structures for the performer. For the audience, this is the most challenging type of jazz to listen to and requires the most active interpretation and

Table 4.3 Types of improvisational contexts[21]

S T R U C T U R E				
	Hi	**High Structure/Low Risk** Examples: – Traditional jazz music – Business simulations	**High Structure/High Risk** Examples: – Surgical procedures – Military operations	
	Lo	**Low Structure/Low Risk** Examples: – "Free" jazz music – Free form brainstorming	**Low Structure/High Risk** Examples: – Emergency management – Fixing the world financial system	
		Lo	Hi	
		Magnitude of Consequences		

sense-making. Both are considered low risk in that the consequences of a poor choice are minimal. While it may result in embarrassment to the performer and some dismay on the part of the listeners, these "damages" are temporary and easily recovered from. Other low-risk environments include most forms of the performing arts (although dance could result in physical injury), the visual and literary arts (although inflammatory material can carry civil and criminal penalties), and simulations used in business, engineering, and health care. Lower MoC contexts encourage decision makers to take risks of increasing magnitude and to push the envelope of what is "expected." We see this occurring in jazz on a frequent basis. It also appears that people who are submerged in gaming environments and simulated worlds like Second Life may assume more risk in the context of the game because the consequences are virtual.

High-risk environments are typical in business, medicine, and engineering practice, such as emergency management (EM), crisis management, complex surgical procedures, and logistics. In these cases, poor decisions can result in physical, psychological, and financial harm to one or more stakeholders[22]. Although some high-risk contexts such as doing complex surgeries or executing a military missions benefit from a fair degree of problem structure, they are nonetheless risky.

High-risk contexts typically constrain decision makers, who will be more cautious and attempt to rely on existing routines. This is typical when doing complex surgical procedures. The surgeon and his or her team will adhere to well-constructed protocols and routines; deviation is not desirable unless absolutely necessary. This type of improvisation is different, becoming the "flexible treatment of pre-planned material"[23]

However, decision makers may be forced to improvise given a deficit of knowledge or experience or both.

Antecedents of Improvisation

There are several antecedent conditions that lead to opportunities for improvisation. These include but are not limited to the following:

- Unexpected problems
- New or revised goals

- Changes in the structure of the problem space
- Changes in the environment
- Knowledge limitations

Problems that emerge unexpectedly can trigger improvisational behaviors by the agents. The case of Apollo 13 dramatically illustrates the role of antecedent conditions. The explosion in the fuel line of the spacecraft sent the crew and ground support group into a frenzy of improvised problem-solving. In Table 4.4 we see how the values of these factors changed.

The onset the explosion imposed severe time constraints on the decision makers because the lives of the crew depended on swift diagnosis and treatment. The structure of the problem space abruptly changed from "routine" to "novel" because of the unspecified damage to the ship. There were now limited structures or routines available to help. The state of knowledge went from relatively complete to incomplete. The crew now found itself in a turbulent environment[24] of multiple interconnected problems. Goals were quickly revised in order to survive. The crew thus went from performing a relatively routine set of activities such as research projects and deployment to a mode of improvisation in order to survive. They had to very quickly diagnose the problem and craft a strategy to deal with the new goal of returning to Earth. They developed new solutions based on existing knowledge and constructed hypotheses on the spot because they had no choice.

Table 4.4 *Illustration of the change in antecedent conditions in case of apollo 13*[25]

Condition	Before	After
Unexpected problems	None	Numerous
Structure of the problem space	Well known	Limited structures or routines
New or revised goals	No	Yes
The environment	Stable	Turbulent
Knowledge limitations	Well-articulated base of knowledge	Limited or no knowledge by agents
Constraints	Within range	Time and resource constrains

Although transitions from high-structure/high-risk situations to low-structure/high-risk contexts rarely occur so dramatically, there is considerable variation in terms of the degree of improvisation over the course of a performance. In other words, whether the context changes or not, the degree of improvisation is not static and may change over a given time period (i.e., during performance).

Levels of Improvisation

At its simplest level, improvisation is a set of design or problem-solving behaviors that involve the modification of a *referent*. A referent is knowledge of processes and procedures that guide and constrains an improviser's choices. For example, a referent can be a score or a set of procedures, routines, or scripts. In business, it can be a *standard operating procedure* (SOP), in medicine a *protocol*, and in music a *score*.

There is considerable difference between what is referred to as an "improvisation" in one context versus another. Those differences are the consequence of the degree to which the referent is modified by the improviser and we can discern at least five different categories of improvisation (see Figure 4.1):

- Replication (i.e., no improvisation)
- Interpretation
- Embellishment
- Variation
- Improvisation (i.e., full improvisation)

Replication indicates there is no change in the referent. Replication is just a simple copying of the original with all its structural and functional features intact. *Interpretation* involves subtle changes to the referent. This is evidenced by conductors who interpret a work by Bach or Mozart. The score or "instruction set" is given and meant to be replicated but with slight stylistic changes by the orchestra leader, thus giving rise to a characteristic sound of a particular orchestra; for example, the Philadelphia Orchestra under Eugene Ormandy.

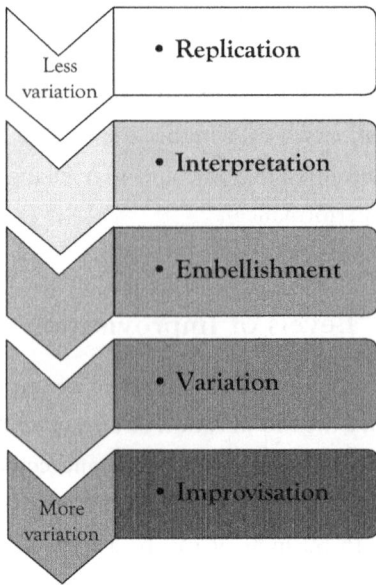

Figure 4.1 Levels of improvisation

Embellishment is an active and purposive act of changing the referent, but within well-defined boundaries imposed by the genre. Embellishments typically enhance the major qualities of the referent by reinforcing them and accentuating them rather than diminishing them. A cartoonist or storyteller embellishes to highlight certain features of the image or storyline. A *variation* is an active modification of the original referent to achieve a certain effect. The variation may accent certain feature and diminish others all the while keeping the identity and coherence of the original form.

Finally, an *improvisation* encourages the participant to modify all structural and functional features of the referent under certain guidelines imposed by the domain. In jazz music, these are the rules of harmony and rhythm. The improviser is careful to make modifications that still retain the outline and identify of the original, even if those boundaries are tenuous. The difference between staying "in" or going "out" in jazz is a measure of how far the improviser strays from the referent. In EM situations, the improviser is still aware of key social and technical rules and boundaries that constrain choices as modifications are made to procedures and routines.

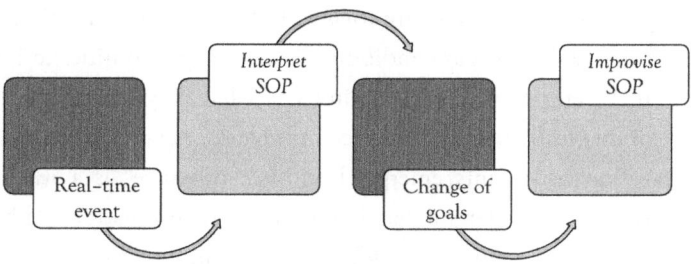

Figure 4.2 Milestones during improvisational performances

The Performance Aspects of Improvisation

Improvisation is about performance. A *performance* is a finite period of time during which a person executes a sequence of actions. In music, this would include the beginning, middle, and end of a concert piece or song. In an EM context, it would be the onset of the crisis, containment, and the transition to a noncrisis or routine state.

Improvisational performances are situated in time between an *initialization* phase and an *epilog* phase. In the initialization phase, members agree on a referent and other parameters of performance. The epilog phase occurs at the completion or near completion of the performance. The epilog is the final opportunity for new ideas, modification of referent, or closing pattern. In music this is referred to as a *cadenza*.

Each performance is thus a unique *realization* of the referent. The performance may contain episodes of improvisation alternating with the performance of scripts and routines based on changes in conditions or the goals of the agents. See Figure 4.2.

Summary of What It Means to Improvise

Let me summarize what has been stated in the previous sections of the chapter.

Unlike the popular notions of improvisation, improvisation is a skill that can be developed through practice, discipline, and education. To become a great improviser requires mastery of the domain's language; that is, the words and sentences that make up the domain. In jazz, this is rhythm and harmony. In EM, it is the policies and procedures that enable first responders to save lives. Improvisers learn to modify the referents in their respective domains as conditions warrant. Opportunities to improvise occur when people reach the limits of what they know, conditions change dramatically due to unforeseen problems, new goals are selected, and real-time constraints emerge. Each "performance" is a *realization* or variation of the referent that is unique to that situation. Although improvisation can occur at the individual level, much of it occurs in the context of teams. In *Designing Creative High Power Teams and Organizations: Beyond Leadership*, which is also available through Business Expert Press, we look at how teams improvise, and what other conditions are necessary for them to be effective.

Developing Your Improvisational Capacity

Improvisation is a skill like any other and can be learned. Let's apply the P3 approach to developing your improvisational capacity.

Prepare

The first step in the process is to pick a domain. What do you wish to improvise in? You will need to immerse yourself in the history development of the field, the rules of the domain, and the vocabulary of "words" that can be voiced. Improvisation is like learning a language. You begin by learning the words that can be formed into sentences to articulate a complete performance. A performance is a unique sequence of words and sentences. You also need to develop an understanding of "deep" knowledge about the domain such as experts have. In jazz music, much of the learning takes place by listening to jazz masters, copying solos, and later incorporating their vocabulary into one's solos in unique ways.

Practice

Once you have picked a domain and studied its fundamentals you need to practice. Practice is in the form of learning words, sentences, and patterns that can be "spoken" in real time. Let me give some examples.

In jazz music there are numerous patterns that can be earned using the 12 notes of the scale. Hundreds. Thousands. Originally transmitted through oral tradition, whole books have been written today that document these patterns. Aspiring players practice these patterns until they gain proficiency. They also copy the patterns developed by the masters as noted earlier. Learning harmonic theory (i.e., what melodies work with particular foundations) and compositional forms are also important.

In Tango, the dancer learns basic steps that can be combined during performance to render a unique sequence of dance "words, sentences, and paragraphs." Unlike other dance forms that may include very difficult but repetitive patterns of footwork, Tango dancers learn sets of words and sentences that are varied according to the music and the whim of the dancers.

In military operations, members of the group drill extensively in routines regarding fighting, logistics, communication, and so forth. They become so adept at these patterns that they can modify them to meet changes in conditions as necessary. Use the same approach to practice improvisation in your areas of interest.

Perform

Our next step is to take this knowledge and skill base into real-time settings starting with ones that have low risk and proceeding to ones that have higher risk as proficiency is attained (see Table 4.3). In jazz, newer performers play with other people at the same or slightly higher levels to practice patterns and routines. In the process they learn ways to communicate with other musicians to enable improvisation to take place in an integrated way. Similarly, a triage team will practice routines together so as to enable them to improvise when necessary in real time. Connection, trust, and coordination are essential elements to team improvisation. For those interested in learning more about team improvisation and building creative high power teams and organizations, the reader is referred to *Designing Creative High Power Teams and Organizations: Beyond Leadership*, which is also available through Business Expert Press.

Chapter Summary

The ability to improvise is a skill that is vital to personal, team, and organizational development. While following the script and employing knowledge reuse is fine for certain contexts, dramatic changes in conditions will warrant modification of the referent. Improvisation occurs when any alteration of the referent pattern occurs in real time. This ranges from embellishment to interpretation to variation to full improvisation. Improvisers in all fields work with the "words" and other patterns that populate the domain. Ironically, the more you practice patterns, the more adept you will become as an improviser.

Improvisation occurs in four different contexts: low structure/low risk; high structure/low risk; low structure/high risk; low structure/high risk. Examples include jazz musicians, surgical teams, flight crews, and entrepreneurs, to name a few. Investing in improvisational capacity is critical for all organizations and can ensure survival in life and death situations. Apollo 13 is a case in point as is U.S. Airways Flight 1549. Organizations need more Captain Sullenbergers in their ranks.

CHAPTER 5

Develop Your Design Proficiency

Design is the fundamental soul of a human-made creation that ends up expressing itself in successive outer layers of the product or service.
—Steve Jobs, CEO, Apple Computer

Design is where science and art break even.
—Robin Mathew, designer

All architecture is shelter, all great architecture is the design of space that contains, cuddles, exalts, or stimulates the persons in that space.
—Philip Johnson, architect

Design is another form of competitive advantage for individuals and organizations. Surprised? You shouldn't be. The emergence of design as a leading area of research in business began years ago. What is design? What can you do to develop your design abilities? In this chapter we will explore the meaning of design and ways to cultivate it.

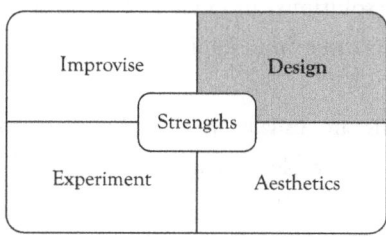

What Is Design?

Design like many "grand" ideas, has a variety of meanings. Let's begin with the dictionary[1] definition of design:

- To conceive or fashion in the mind; invent.
- To formulate a plan for; devise: design a marketing strategy for the new product.
- To plan out in systematic, usually graphic form: design a building; design a computer program.
- To create or contrive for a particular purpose or effect: a game designed to appeal

What can we learn from the statements above? First, we recognize that design is a particular instance of creative behavior.[2] Second, the outputs of this behavior are tangible in some way; for example, a plan, a product, a game, a process, a building, and so forth. Third, designs emerge in the context of a need, which implies a consumer or recipient. Fourth, design is deliberate and structured. Design requires discipline.

Design been described as the passage from a functional description to a physical description of an artifact.[3] More broadly, some argue that design is a form of problem solving. What kind of problems? Not all, but a majority of design efforts involve the solution of *ill-structured problems*. In general, problems range from structured to ill-structured.[4] A structured problem is easily recognized, has a clear and finite set of solutions, and can be represented. Ill-structured problems are not easily framed, have many possible solutions, and may not be easily represented. Innovative design problems oftentimes fall into the latter category.

> Design problems are usually among the most complex and ill-structured kinds of problems that are encountered in practice. For many years, researchers (Reitman, 1965; Simon, 1973) have characterized design problems as ill-structured because they have ambiguous specification of goals, no determined solution path, and the need to integrate multiple knowledge domains. Whether it is an electronic circuit, a house, a new entree for a restaurant, a musical composition, an

essay, or any other product or system, designing requires applying general and domain-specific schemas as well as procedural knowledge.[5]

Design problems do not have a clear right or wrong answer, just varying degrees of satisfaction:

Why are design problems so ill-structured? Goel and Pirolli (1989) articulated the characteristics of design problems, including many degrees of freedom in the problem statement, which consists only of goals and intentions, limited or delayed feedback from the world, artifacts as outputs that must function independently of the designer, and answers that tend to be neither right nor wrong, only better or worse.[6]

Here is the working definition of design that we shall use throughout this book:

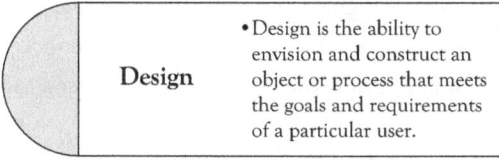

Design · Design is the ability to envision and construct an object or process that meets the goals and requirements of a particular user.

Design Contexts

Examples of design and designed artifacts are found in a variety of fields, including classical music, architecture, engineering, software, graphic design, and product design as indicated in Table 5.1.

For example, ballet, opera, and classical music are all products of design. The design is codified in the form of a score or a script. Even comedy shows[7] are scripted, despite the appearance of being spontaneous or "off the cuff." Finished works of art are the outcome of planning and design. For example, when Rodin sculpted some of his most famous works, he did so after having sketched and completed various studies first. You may not think of writing as a product of design or problem solving, but it is:

Expert writers, for instance, are problem solvers who exert tremendous "mental effort in the elaboration, the coordination, and the

Table 5.1 Examples of design in various fields

Area	Sub-area	Design outcomes
Performing arts	Music	Classical music
	Theater	Opera
	Dance	Ballet
	Comedy	Comedy shows
Visual arts		Finished works of art
Literary arts		Novels, poems, essays
Engineering		Buildings, products, bridges
Management		New product development, for example, the iPhone
Social contexts		Organizational design, city planning, community design

execution of complex goals and sub goals, such as how to shape content for a particular audience, how to express conceptual intentions in the language of prose, or how to construct a catchy title"[8]

Certainly, buildings, bridges, and other structures are products of design process. Finally, products such as the iPhone emerged only after extensive research, design, testing, prototyping, and review.

Like improvisation, there are several design contexts based on risk and the structure of the problem space (see Table 5.2). Unlike improvisational contexts, there are few real-time constraints; that is, actions are not necessarily taken in real time and can extend over hours, days, months, or years.

Design contexts are classified according to (1) risk of failure (i.e., the magnitude of consequences) and (2) the problem structure. Designing a print advertisement or a standard computer are highly structured problems because of the enormous experience we have with such tasks. They are considered low risk since the worst outcomes typically are financial risk or impacting someone's reputation.

Designing new products such as Facebook are not only low risk but also lower structure problems because we have less experience with social

Table 5.2 Types of design contexts

		Lo	Hi
S T R U C T U R E	**Hi**	**High Structure/Low Risk** Examples: – Designing a print advertisement – Designing computer systems	**High Structure/High Risk** Examples: – Designing a bridge – Designing a power plant

	Lo	**Low Structure/Low Risk**
		Examples:
		– Designing a new social net-
		  working service
		– Designing a new search service
		  (e.g., Google)
			Low Structure/High Risk
			Examples:
			– Designing a new transportation
			  system (e.g., Boston's Big Dig)
			– Designing a new health-care
			  system

Magnitude of Consequences

networking software than say word processing software. Designing a bridge or a nuclear power plant is a high-risk design task but one that is highly structured. The most challenging design problems are low structure *and* high risk. These include building new transportation systems such as Boston's Big Dig or a new health-care system because of the immense complexity of such tasks. Failure in this case can lead to loss of life and so the risk is considered high.

What Designers Do

Designers, like all creative people, *influence* others through the works they produce. Gardner[9] defines a creator as someone who *creates on a regular basis, fashioning ideas, concepts and objects in a given domain in new and novel ways that are ultimately accepted by the community* of which they are a part. Creators thus lead others indirectly through the symbols they manipulate (e.g., language, mathematics, images) and the works that they produce. Great designers appear in all fields and a few are shown in Table 5.3.

Leonardo da Vinci, a Renaissance man, was a master of several disciplines. He was versed as a painter, sculptor, architect, musician, scientist,

Table 5.3 Examples of great designers[10]

Leonardo da Vinci (artist)	Thomas Edison (inventor)	Frank Gehry (architect)
Tim Berners-Lee[11] (scientist—CERN)	Jane Austen (writer)	Jonathan Ive[12] (designer—Apple)

mathematician, engineer, inventor, anatomist, geologist, cartographer, botanist, and writer. Born in 1452, his painted works include the Mona Lisa and The Last Supper. In addition to his works as an artist, da Vinci made contributions to science through his study of the properties of light, air, rocks, and fossils. He applied his artistic talents and powers of observation to the study of the human body and the bodies of birds, thus making a contribution to the field of anatomy. He also designed several artifacts including military barricades, large-span bridges, helicopters, and hang gliders to name a few. Unlike most gifted people, he made significant contributions to several fields.

Thomas Edison was born in 1847 and was one of America's greatest inventors. In addition to inventing the light bulb, he also developed the phonograph, the stock ticker, and the motion picture camera. Unlike many inventors, he was also an entrepreneur. He helped champion the concept of distributing electric power to homes and businesses, and was an advocate for mass production to lower costs. Several companies were an outgrowth of his work including Edison General Electric, which merged with Thomson-Houston Electric Company to form General Electric, and Commonwealth Edison, which is now part of Exelon, among others. His thus made transformative contributions to the fields of power, lighting, and music distribution and imaging.

Frank Gehry is one of my favorites and is considered one of the best architects in the world. His architectural designs contain the cast of Disney, great works of art in the Guggenheim museum located in Bilbao, Spain, corporate offices in the United States, and scientists in Las Vegas searching for a cure to Alzheimer's. His designs are bold, startling, refreshing, and whimsical; some appear to defy gravity. He renders organic forms with high-tech materials to articulate spaces in unique and daring ways. In short, his designs are gorgeous and unmistakable. Born in 1929, his works span several decades and appear throughout the world.

Jane Austen was a novelist who lived in the period 1775–1817. Her major works included *Sense and Sensibility, Pride and Prejudice, Mansfield Park* and *Emma*. Because she published anonymously during her lifetime, she received little recognition for her literary designs until the 20th century. Scholars have since declared her one of the great writers of English fiction because of probing insights into the upper class, morality, class, women's rights, marriage, and education. Although she lived a short life, her works have endured in the form of books, movies, and documentaries.

Tim Berners-Lee web page[13] appropriately reads:

A graduate of Oxford University, Tim Berners-Lee invented the World Wide Web, an Internet-based hypermedia initiative for global information sharing while at CERN, the European Particle Physics Laboratory, in 1989. He wrote the first web client and server in 1990. His specifications of URLs, HTTP, and HTML were refined as Web technology spread.

That about says it all. His work at CERN, in trying to help scientists share data, led to the development of the World Wide Web and the rest as we say is history. According to Internetworldstats.com,[14] the number of people using the Web is well over *2 billion* and includes all the major continents of the world. Growth from 2000 to 2012 was 566%. The web has connected the world in ways not dreamed possible before and has had as much impact as the advent of the printing press. Talk about the influence of a design.

Jonathan Ive has been described as "the man who, after Jobs, is most responsible for Apple's amazing ability to dazzle and delight with

Table 5.4 Statistics on Apple (9/22/2012)[17]

Apple products sold	Total units sold
iPod	350,000,000
iPhone	192,600,000
iPad	84,000,000
Apple TV	2,400,000
Macintosh computers (both desktop and laptop)	212,000,000
Total number of Apple Stores	361
iTunes songs downloaded	16.5 billion
Total number of iPhone App Store downloads	2 billion

its famous products..."[15] Born in 1967 in London, he is without a doubt one of the most influential industrial designers in the world. He joined Apple in 1992 and serves as Senior VP of Industrial Design. He was termed the "smartest designer" by Fortune magazine in 2010.[16] He has been responsible for translating former CEO Job's vision for the iPod, the iPhone, and the iPad into sound product design. His work has been wildly successful and is a major reason for Apple's success. A snapshot of product sales of some of the designs he oversaw is shown in Table 5.4.

Types of Designers

Designers (and all creators for that matter) range from *masters* to *makers*.[18] A master is someone who thoroughly exhausts the possibilities of a genre such that there is very little that can be added without changing the boundaries significantly. Mozart is one such example. He so thoroughly explored the Baroque and early classical harmonies and musical elements of his day that others were forced to change the rules and boundaries to have something meaningful to say. Those that followed him such as Beethoven (late classical) and Brahms (early Romantic) experimented with different harmonies and musical textures to create works that distinguished them from prior compositions. In a sense, the later composers had to *remake* the domain in order to compete. Howard Gardner calls these creators *makers*.

The history of the fields of design (e.g., art, architecture, music, art, etc.) is filled with examples of masters giving way to makers. In physics, Newton's ideas gave way to Einstein's, who was a maker of the new domain of relativity. Niels Bohr then later redefined physics in terms of quantum mechanics. Martha Graham remade the world of dance. Cirque du Soleil redefined the circus experience. Filmmakers such as Ridley Scott redefined the science-fiction genre. Charlie Parker and John Coltrane redefined the boundaries of jazz music and playing the saxophone, as did Miles Davis whose musical compositions and recordings are unparalleled. Picasso and other cubists redefined our way of seeing three-dimensional objects. Apple Computer redefined how users interact with computers by bringing the mouse and graphical user interface to mass market.[19] Apple has continued to redefine how users interact with their music (iPod), their phones (iPhone), and more recently their social networks via the iPad. Masters and makers thus populate all fields of art, design, and production.

Characteristics of Designers

What does it take to be a good designer? All human beings are naturally gifted as designers, and much better at design than say decision making. "Human agents have a surprising and infinitely expandable ability to create stories, forms, and concepts."[20] We augment our abilities through three processes: (1) we learn to manipulate existing concepts and expand the set of concepts; (2) we develop prototypes and mock-ups; (3) we engage in multi-stakeholder processes of social interaction to enhance the designs.[21]

Tim Brown, the CEO of Ideo, believes that good designers are "T-shaped."[22] T-shaped people have a core area of expertise (aligned along the vertical leg) as well as an ability (and desire) to collaborate across disciplines (aligned along the horizontal axis). In his own words:

The horizontal stroke of the "T" is the disposition for collaboration across disciplines. It is composed of two things. First, empathy. It's important because it allows people to imagine the problem from another perspective- to stand in somebody else's shoes.

Second, they tend to get very enthusiastic about other people's disciplines, to the point that they may actually start to practice them. T-shaped people have both depth and breadth in their skills.[23]

While the vertical and horizontal skills noted by Brown are important, I would argue that human beings need several characteristics to make them successful as designers. These include general and specific areas of multiple intelligence strengths as shown in Table 5.5.

To begin, a good designer needs to have the ability to focus or even develop an obsession with the object of his or her design. One of the most successful tent designers, David Mydans (from the well-known outdoor sporting goods company REI), was described this way:[24]

Mydans, who has been designing products since 1986 is a self-described "dirtbag climbing bum," a scraggly graybeard who spends upward of sixty days every year sleeping in a tent. "I like to lie in a tent late in the afternoon, when the sun is low in the sky, and see the architecture of the tent," he says.

Table 5.5 Success factors for designers

Areas of strength	Design abilities
General	• Mental focus • Persistence • Flexibility • Enthusiasm
Interpersonal intelligence	• Listening skills • Empathetic understanding
Visual–spatial intelligence	• Ability to see in multiple dimensions
Mathematical–logical intelligence	• Planning • Structuring • Encoding
Bodily kinesthetic intelligence	• Prototyping
Verbal–linguistic intelligence	• Communication skills
Intrapersonal intelligence	• Self-awareness regarding beliefs, values, and thought processes
Other	• Improvisational skills • Aesthetic awareness

He obsessed over making the company's Quarter Dome tent larger yet lighter. Many sketches later, "obsessive tinkering," a prototype, and a successful wind tunnel test at 25 miles per hour, the final product won the Editor's Choice award from backpacker magazine in 2006 and sales improved 162%. David Mydans later said, "Necessity is the mother of expediency. Obsession is the mother of invention."[25]

The flip side of the necessary focus and persistence is an ability to be flexible. Contradiction? Not really. Designers must experiment to get the design right. If something is not working, then sometimes the best alternative is to simply move on to a new variation. Good designers know when to temper persistence with flexibility. Furthermore, a good designer is able to adapt to changes in the specifications as the product or service evolves. What may have worked at first glance may not represent the ultimate solution. Kitchenware maker, OXO spent eight years "perfecting" a design for a travel mug, which nearly failed several times before the final design emerged. Persistence and flexibility kept the project going until it finally proved to be successful.[26]

Another key attribute of a good designer is an ability to empathize and to listen, really listen. In the final analysis, the designer must create an *authentic* experience for the user. To create that experience, the designer must deeply understand the needs and wants of the user. He or she must live the product from the user's perspective. This is a critical interpersonal strength.

Designers must also be good at perception in the world and in the mind's eye. They need to develop a heightened sense of aesthetic awareness and be able to take in and analyze data provided by the senses. They also need to cultivate the ability to imagine how things look (and feel) in three dimensions. This skill is especially important as they develop prototypes. They need to "see" how things might look and then have the discipline to construct mock-ups of designs. The latter may require bodily kinesthetic skills to fashion artifacts, such as cars, sets, clothes, and so forth. The work of proto-typing and production requires planning and structuring skills.

They may also need to improvise as they face challenges not foreseen at the outset. A wonderful example of the interplay between planned and improvised is provided in the example of Boston's Big Dig. During this massive highway and bridge project planned over decades, architects and designers were faced with improvising solutions to various unforeseen problems such as soil stabilization, floating building platforms, and freezing huge sections of earth to aid in drilling. Without an ability to improvise, the project would never have been completed.

Finally, designers embed their values in their works. To do so requires them to know what those values and core beliefs are; that is, they need a certain degree of interpersonal intelligence to know who they are and what they (and their designs) stand for.

The Experience of Design and Creation

What does it feel to be a creator and a designer? To really excel as a designer you need to live it and really immerse yourself in the creation just as David Mydans did. What is this state? How is it characterized? The work of Mihaly Csikszentmihalyi, Professor of Psychology and Management at Claremont University, is instructive in this regard. Csikszentmihalyi has studied the internal states of artists, athletes, designers, and business people for decades. Those moments identified with total immersion in the act of creation he defines as *flow*. Flow is a state in which the individual transcends him or herself and flows through time like water (see for example Figure 5.1). The characteristics are shown in Table 5.6.

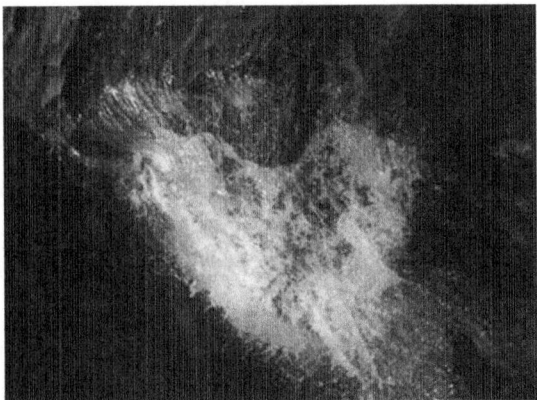

Figure 5.1 "Triumphant splash"[28]

Table 5.6 Characteristics of flow[27]

1. **There are clear goals every step of the way**. Knowing what you are trying to achieve gives your actions a sense of purpose and meaning.
2. **There is immediate feedback to your actions**. Not only do you know what you are trying to achieve, you are also clear about how well you are doing it. This makes it easier to adjust for optimum performance. It also means that flow only occurs when you are performing well.
3. **There is a balance between challenges and skills**. If the challenge is too difficult we get frustrated; if it is too easy, we get bored. Flow occurs when we reach an optimum balance between our abilities and the task in hand, keeping us alert, focused and effective.
4. **Action and awareness are merged**. We have all had experiences of being in one place physically, but with our minds elsewhere often out of boredom or frustration. In flow, we are completely focused on what we are doing in the moment.
5. **Distractions are excluded from consciousness**. When we are not distracted by worries or conflicting priorities, we are free to become fully absorbed in the task.
6. **There is no worry of failure**. A single-minded focus of attention means that we are not simultaneously judging our performance or worrying about things going wrong.
7. **Self-consciousness disappears**. When we are fully absorbed in the activity itself, we are not concerned with our self-image, or how we look to others. While flow lasts, we can even identify with something outside or larger than our sense of self such as the painting or writing we are engaged in, or the team we are playing in.
8. **The sense of time becomes distorted**. Several hours can fly by in what feels like a few minutes, or a few moments can seem to last for ages.
9. **The activity becomes 'autotelic'—meaning it is an end in itself**. Whenever most of the elements of flow are occurring, the activity becomes enjoyable and rewarding for its own sake. This is why so many artists and creators report that their greatest satisfaction comes through their work.

His research has found that very few people engage in this state, esp. in the workplace. More likely we experience anxiety, boredom, or apathy. According to Csikszentmihalyi,[29] there are at least eight different states of being that we experience based on the match between our skills and the challenges posed by the task environment. Too much challenge and we become anxious. Too little challenge and we are bored. Somewhere in between, we experience control or arousal. When the balance is just right, we experience flow (see Figure 5.2).

All great creators access this state, sometimes out of necessity. Here is a short anecdote about Ray Bradbury, the great science fiction writer who attained flow to such a level that he wrote one of his most famous novels in under 10 days.

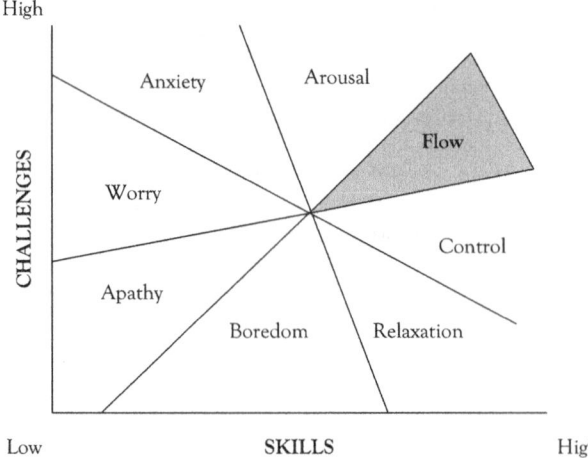

Figure 5.2 States of being based on the match between skills and challenges[30]

On January 5, 2005, Dana Gioia, former Chairman of the National Endowment for the Arts, interviewed Ray Bradbury in Los Angeles. An excerpt from their conversation follows.

Dana Gioia: How did you come to write Fahrenheit 451?

Ray Bradbury: In 1950, our first baby was born, and in 1951, our second, so our house was getting full of children. It was very loud, it was very wonderful, but I had no money to rent an office. I was wandering around the UCLA library and discovered there was a typing room where you could rent a typewriter for ten cents a half-hour. So I went and got a bag of dimes. The novel began that day, and nine days later it was finished. But my God, what a place to write that book! I ran up and down stairs and grabbed books off the shelf to find any kind of quote and ran back down and put it in the novel. The book wrote itself in nine days.[31]

Bradbury was clearly in flow. He was surrounded by the things he loved: a quiet space, books, and a typewriter. As creators and designers, our goal is to access this state. As leaders and managers, our goal is to encourage this state.

Develop Your Design Proficiency

Prepare

Did you know that there are over 60 D-Schools around the world? What is a D-School? Since 2007, Businessweek has published a list of the top design, engineering and business schools that offer a strong emphasis in design.[32] What do you need to learn to become a designer?

At Carnegie Mellon University, students are immersed in the subjects listed in Table 5.7 in the Master of Design in Communication Planning and Information Design.

Carnegie also has a Masters of Product Development that is ranked in the top 5 according to U.S. News and World Report, which has the following curriculum shown in Table 5.8.

To become an effective designer, you need to master certain skills. First, you must understand the *vocabulary* of the chosen domain. *All* design takes place in a specific domain of knowledge. Learning to design "in general" is a meaningless statement. You must immerse yourself in

Table 5.7 Design curriculum at Carnegie Mellon University

Area	Description
Design context	How design relates to human interactions
Design studio	Learning how to visualize complex information
Narrative and argument	Workshop in writing in various communicaton forms
Protoyping	Practice in the art of constructing prototypes
Design research methods	Study of the use of various research methods in the profession
Graduate thesis	Application of design to solve a particular problem or need

Table 5.8 Carnegie Mellon's master of product development[33]

Semester I	Semester II
Industrial Design Fundamentals	Integrated Product Development
Engineering Design Fundamentals	Market Research
Design For Manufacture	Product Planning
Visualization: a Process Tool	Elective
User Research Methods	Elective
Innovation and Entrepreneurship	–

the ideas, concepts, and tools of the domain; for example, information systems, consumer products, travel services, and so forth. Vocabulary is contained in the bite-sized solutions or patterns that are developed and from which larger more complex designs are built from. The concept of design patterns is prevalent in the field. A design pattern is a solution that has proven to provide certain functions and to satisfy certain needs. Patterns are useful because they obviate the need to redesign the wheel.

You also need to exercise your imagination. Learning to let your mind go to generate and explore new ideas is fundamental to the design process. Tamping down on the voice of judgment is an important skill.

Practice

Design is a function of doing. Much of it is learned in the process of designing. For this reason, most programs have opportunities to apply design principles to a particular domain. Fundamental to the design process is prototyping and producing mock-ups of the design. Imagination can only take you so far. It is important to be able to render the essential elements of the design in some concrete form. In software, it can be the mock-up of a Web page layout. In the auto industry, it would involve sculpting body designs in clay or laying out the instrumentation on a computer simulation. Visualization is a critical skill of the design process and developing your visual intelligence as well as visualization is found in most design programs.

Perform

In summary, the best way to practice design is to do it. Redesign your life. Your work. A product you use that doesn't work well. Write stories. Construct models. Compose music. Imagine. Identify functions. Create forms. Prototype. Build.

Chapter Summary

Design is a critical creative skill and tests our ability to solve complex ill-structured problems. It appears in all areas of life: art, music, the workplace, products, services, writing, and many others. Designers have come to shape the world we live in, from the marvels of great architects like Frank Geary to the devices we use like the iPhone to the music we play, to the workplaces and communities we inhabit. In each of these fields, masters give way to makers. Designers fashion their ideas into concrete artifacts on a regular basis; seldom are they done after one work. They usually spend a lifetime in their chosen field and oftentimes get better at it over time.

Becoming a designer requires several skills ranging from mental focus and persistence to empathy for the user, to an ability to visualize and construct prototypes. Designers must be self-aware and not be afraid to take risks, improvise, or exercise aesthetic judgments. Designers, and all creators for that matter, experience flow, a heightened state of immersion where time stands still, ego is dissipated, and there is a general feeling of well-being.

Learning to become a designer may occur on the job but there are many opportunities to gain proficiency in design by attending one of nearly 60 D-Schools around the world. You can also develop your design proficiency on your own through exercises and practice in a particular domain of knowledge.

CHAPTER 6

Expand Your Scientific and Experimental Mind

No amount of experimentation can ever prove me right; a single experiment can prove me wrong.

—Albert Einstein, scientist

Evening is a time of real experimentation. You never want to look the same way.

—Donna Karan, fashion designer

I am enough of an artist to draw freely upon my imagination. Imagination is more important than knowledge. Knowledge is limited. Imagination encircles the world.

—Albert Einstein, scientist

Overview

You may be wondering why the topics of science and experimentation appear in a book on creativity. Most people fear science and view it as far away from creative activity as possible. In reality, science is one of the most creative endeavors of the human mind. Your scientific mind helps you to understand the natural world and by doing so, you attain many valuable skills. To understand the nature of the world that we inhabit, we begin with observation. Truly observing the world is a skill in and of itself. From observations we develop mental models of the world based on notions of association, causality, inference, and so forth. The formation of mental models allows us to exercise our imagination. Those mental models must be subjected to tests to determine their efficacy. We do this via experiments. Experimentation is the cornerstone of science. The history of science is a history of great thinkers and the models they developed, tested, and either clung to or reformulated.

Your scientific mind teaches you to be nimble, flexible, rigorous, structured, imaginative, and tenacious. You also learn to defend your ideas verbally and in print. Science is not for the faint of heart. It takes guts to defend your mental models and to convince others of their efficacy. After all, we are talking about models that pertain to the *nature of reality.*

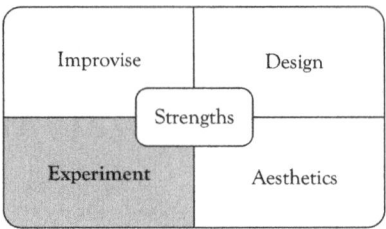

Defining Science

So what is science? According to the *Academic Press Dictionary of Science and Technology,*[1] science is:

1. The systematic observation of natural events and conditions in order to discover facts about them and to formulate laws and principles based on these facts.
2. The organized body of knowledge that is derived from such observations and that can be verified or tested by further investigation.
3. Any specific branch of this general body of knowledge, such as biology, physics, geology, or astronomy.

Put another way, science is about the discovery of patterns and the underlying order that appears to be woven through the fabric of the natural world.

> Science is an intellectual activity carried on by humans that is designed to discover information about the natural world in which humans live and to discover the ways in which this information can be organized into meaningful patterns. ... An ultimate purpose of science is to discern the order that exists between and amongst the various facts.[2]

Our best understanding of the nature of the world and nonliving systems comes from the disciplines of physics, chemistry, and the earth sciences. Knowledge gained from these disciplines is also based on mental models, frameworks, and assumptions.[3] Historically, the physical sciences have experienced several revolutions in thought over the centuries. The primary mental models that have been developed in the fields of physics and mathematics are identified in Table 6.1.

There are several reasons to study the evolution of scientific thinking. First, we get a firsthand look at several mental models that have shaped the ways human beings have thought about nature over the past two thousand years. Each model is represented by a Thinker type (see Table 6.1). Second, the models themselves give evidence of the imagination of scientists, coupled with rigorous observation and testing.

Third, remnants of these models coexist today within your own mental models of reality. It is important to see the advantages, and limitations, of these models. Some models support the expression of creative activity while others do not. It is important to see how these mental models may be helping or hindering your journey toward creative expression. For instance, the Intuitive Thinker holds very different assumptions than the Deterministic Thinker. Knowing which mental model exerts the most influence on your thinking is critical to becoming a creative person.

Table 6.1 Physical system types and models

Theory/Model	System type	Discovery timeframe	Thinker type
Intuitive/logical	Macroscopic/ microscopic	500 BC to 1700 AD	Intuitive
Newtonian physics	Deterministic-simple	1700–1900	Deterministic
Statistics and probability	Predictive and stochastic systems	1800–1900	Statistical
Chaos theory[4]	Nonlinear systems	1880s and 1960s	Chaotic
Relativity theory	Relativistic systems	1900 to 1920s	Relativistic
Quantum theory	Quantum systems	1930s	Quantum

Fourth, science teaches us to experiment and test our assumptions under structured conditions. Learning to experiment is one of the most useful skills for the creative thinker. For instance, experimentation with thousands of materials led Thomas Edison to discover the optimal material for light bulbs. We need to experiment to grow and develop.

Finally, the history of scientific thinking is one of continual renewal and revolution and shows how even the most creative minds can attach themselves to outdated models. As great a scientist as Einstein was, even he had trouble leaving behind his mental models of the world when confronted with conflicting evidence. He never quite embraced quantum physics (while the rest of world of physics did), which ultimately left him behind. The mental models we carry can exert such a strong influence that even the experiments that we design *can yield the results we are looking for.* In brief, modern physics has forced us to question the meaning of objectivity. The images and models of reality produced by scientists are as striking and novel as any abstract or impressionistic paintings hanging on the walls of the Louvre. Let's look at six scientific models that have shaped human understanding over the past two thousand years. Table 6.2 identifies a key thinker from each school of thought.

Table 6.2 Examples of great scientific thinkers[5]

Intuitive	Deterministic Systems	Statistics
Democritus	Sir Isaac Newton	Blaise Pascal
Chaos Theory	**Relativity**	**Quantum Theory**
Jacques Hadmard	Albert Einstein	Niels Bohr

The Intuitive Thinker

All human knowledge thus begins with intuitions, proceeds thence to concepts, and ends with ideas.

—Immanuel Kant, philosopher

All I am gonna do is just go on and do what I feel.
—Jimi Hendrix, philosopher and musician

The intuitive thinker bases his or her model of the world on intuitive or common sense ideas about how things work. This way of thinking is the most common and has been around the longest. For instance, early conceptions of the universe and the macroscopic world[6] that were developed by the ancient Greeks and Romans had a certain intuitive appeal, but in many cases lacked empirical validation or verification. The ancients also made contributions to astronomy, botany, zoology, earth science, and several areas of applied technology and engineering.

Although hampered by limitations of technology, that did not stop the Greeks from offering insights into the nature of reality at the unseen level or microscopic level (i.e., less than a millimeter). For example, the theory of atoms was first developed by Democritus. He conceived of the world of matter as composed of things he called atoms, derived from the word *atomos*, which means indivisible. Democritus believed that atoms were the smallest components of matter. Although he never saw an atom, it was a logical untested idea that had a certain intuitive appeal. This conceptual model, although flawed, has carried over to modern day (more on this when we discuss quantum physics) and is still taught in primary school.

Another interesting logical and intuitive theory was the theory of the *aether* that appears in Greek mythology. The aether was thought to be the essence that the gods breathed and was identified by Aristotle as a *fifth element*. Hundreds of years later, astronomers and astrophysicists of the 19th century thought that the earth, planets, and stars moved through a sort of cosmic flux referred to as the *ether* or in the case of light, a *luminiferous aether*. This theory was disproved through several experiments, the most famous one being the one carried out by Michelson and Morley in 1887. There are numerous other theories such as the corpuscular model of light and color, Ptolemaic cosmology, the flat earth, and alchemy that we now know are inaccurate or implausible. The point is that even in the hard sciences, theories come and go and may ultimately be proven wrong.

Interestingly, people today who have had limited exposure to science devise all sorts of interesting explanations of physical phenomena. For example, given a scenario of waves passing through a small opening, some people correctly infer a slight bending of the wave. Others do not and imagine the waves stopping or passing through unaltered or even shrinking in size. Like the early Greeks, students creatively invent ways that the world works until confronted by disconfirming evidence. Few understand the cycle of *test–retest–revise* until trained in this type of thinking. Furthermore, another aspect of the models that they have developed often is done so without any thought given to the scope of the model; that is, to what extent does this represent a model that has broad application or is only of limited scope.

In summary, the intuitive thinker bases his or her explanation on common-sense generalizations that probably have not been subjected to rigorous testing by now commonly accepted scientific methods.

The Deterministic Thinker

God does not play dice with the universe.
—Albert Einstein

Life is like a game of cards. The hand you are dealt is determinism; the way you play it is free will.

—Jawaharlal Nehru, statesman

The deterministic thinker views the world as governed by empirically verified laws and rules that offer stability, predictability, and control. The exemplar in this regard is Sir Isaac Newton. Newton was born in 1643 in the town of Woolsthorpe-by-Colsterworth Lincolnshire, England. His father, a farmer, died when Isaac was 3 months old. As a late teen, he went to study at Cambridge University. Over the next 5 years, Newton *discovered* or *invented* branches of mathematics and physics. In mathematics, he discovered the binomial theorem and invented the calculus.

In physics, he made significant contributions to the field of optics as well as astronomy.

In general, Newton's goal was to discover (or invent) simple, elegant laws that had the power to predict the motion of celestial bodies (such as the planets) as well as objects on the earth (such as apples) with high degrees of accuracy. Laws are concisely written as simple mathematical formulas. For instance, the formula $S = vt$ is read to mean, "Distance = velocity times time." So, if we know that we are travelling at 60 miles per hour for 2 hours (uninterrupted), then we can quickly determine that we have gone 120 miles. Of course in the real world, there are all sorts of things that can affect this outcome, such as traffic, running out of gas, stopping to eat, and so forth. However, in a perfect world of bodies in motion, formulas like these correctly and accurately predict outcomes. We call these contexts *simple deterministic systems*. Newton, and others of his time, was concerned about finding formulas such as these that accurately described the world around them, at least the nonhuman world of interaction. In particular, Newton is most famous for discovering the relationship of attraction that occurs between two bodies of considerable weight (or more precisely, mass); that is, his theory of gravity.

$$F \text{ (gravity)} = g \left(M_1 \times M_2 / S^2 \right)$$

This reads that the force of gravity is directly proportional to the mass of object 1 times the mass of object 2 divided by the distance squared (i.e., times itself). The constant "g" makes the numbers work out correctly.

Although Newton had no idea why this formula worked, he could easily calculate the force of attraction between *any* two bodies in the universe. That is a pretty powerful law! This formula has been used to send men to the moon and back, among other things. The wonderful thing about simple deterministic systems is that if you know the values at the start, you can correctly predict the outcome at the end (on the other hand, not all physical systems behave so nicely).

In summary, the Deterministic Thinker understands the world as governed by mathematical laws and rules that have been rigorously tested using scientific methods. With sufficient data, outcomes can be calculated from initial conditions.

The Statistical Thinker

So much of life, it seems to me, is determined by pure randomness.
—Sidney Poitier, actor

Be able to analyze statistics, which can be used to support or undercut almost any argument.
—Marilyn von Savant, author and columnist

It is the mark of a truly intelligent person to be moved by statistics.
—George Bernard Shaw, writer

The Statistical Thinker bases his or her assessment of the nature of the world on probabilities and the analysis and interpretation of large sets of data. Instead of being governed by laws, rules, and equations, the Statistical Thinker prefers probabilities, normal distributions, randomness, and central tendencies. The word statistics means "information about the state of the system." Statistics recognizes that we live in a world with finite time and resources. It is not feasible to collect data on every item, nor is it desirable. For instance, rather than collecting the opinions of all 300 million people in the United States on a survey, we *sample* a subset that we believe represents the whole. This approach saves both time and money. Although values are reported with a confidence interval of say ±5%, we more than make up for this loss of certainty in terms of practicality. Taking this a step further, some scientists assign probabilities to *everything*. Yes, everything. A branch of science known as *fuzzy logic* assigns probabilities to whether your clothes are "dry" (it too is a distribution) to the color "red" to whether you or I can pass through a wall (a nonzero probability). In their eyes, everything has a probability distribution, and mathematically speaking, they are correct. Some of the most famous early statisticians included Gauss, Student, Snedecor, Bienayme, Chebyshev, and Fisher. Pick up any statistics book and you will find hundreds of tests, each associated with a particular scientist.

Statistics is usefully applied to all types of systems. In most cases, we look at the behavior of a particular group relative to what would have occurred by chance. For example, if we wish to know how many people are likely to get in car accidents between the ages of 18 and 25, we can come up with a fairly good estimate of the likelihood based on an analysis of thousands of drivers. This is exactly what insurance companies do in order to set rates for various groups of drivers. You may not think it is fair, but it is statistically accurate and allows insurance companies to make a handsome profit.

Statistics also is concerned about the behavior of systems that cannot be measured directly. For example, we now know that it is impossible to know the exact location of an electron orbiting the nucleus of the atom. This is true for *all atoms in all things in universe.* All we can say is that the electron has a certain probability of being in a certain location at a given time. It is similar to saying that there is certain probability that a cloud is blocking the sun at your location right now. We just don't know. It was hard for physicists to accept this level of uncertainty but the data are so compelling that there was no other choice. More on this issue under quantum physics.

Another system that statisticians study is the stochastic system. The word *stochastic* means "pertaining to chance." Its Greek root is *stochastikos,* which means "proceeding by guesswork."[7] Stochastic systems exhibit random or erratic behavior. For a system to be *stochastic,* one or more parts of the system have randomness associated with it. Unlike a *deterministic* system, for example, a stochastic system does not always produce the same output for a given input. So, if we run an experiment, a process, or even a stochastic machine, the outputs may vary. Stochastic systems are also different from *chaotic systems* (see next section).

In summary, the Stochastic Thinker loves large sets of data so he or she can calculate probabilities of events. He or she utilizes the principles of statistics and probability distributions. Random behavior is a particular source of pleasure. Drawing inferences and making judgments about the world based on the interpretation of historical data is his or her reason for being. The statistician takes pleasure in knowing that a randomly drawn sample saves time and money, yet yields excellent results; results that would make Ben Franklin proud. Statisticians are thus very pragmatic. Unlike the determinist who looks for law-like regularity in the universe, the statistician sees all events as probabilities and is not surprised when things go "wrong." To him, it is inevitable, just as snake eyes at a craps table. Eventually your number comes up.

The Chaotic (Nonlinear) Thinker

Does the flap of a butterfly's wings in Brazil set off a tornado in Texas?
—Edward Lorenz, scientist

Chaos in the world brings uneasiness, but it also allows the opportunity for creativity and growth.
—Tom Barrett, politician

Chaos often breeds life when order breeds habit.
—Henry Adams, statesman

The Chaotic Thinker recognizes that although the world may be based on laws, that many phenomena exhibit wildly different outcomes with small changes in the inputs. These types of systems are called *input-sensitive systems, nonlinear,* or *complex deterministic systems.* Examples of such systems abound in nature from the production of snowflakes (no two are alike) to the behavior of water coming out of a faucet, to intricate patterns that define the coastline, to the formation of weather disturbances such as tornados and storms. The great physicist Murray Gell-Mann put it this way,

> Of course the word chaos is used in rather a vague sense by a lot of writers, but in physics it means a particular phenomenon, namely that in a nonlinear system the outcome is often indefinitely, arbitrarily sensitive to tiny changes in the initial condition.[8]

Chaotic systems were first discovered in the 19th century but were not formalized until the 1960s when computers played a critical role helping scientists to represent and understand chaotic system behavior. Henri Poincare, a French mathematician, was one of the first to formalize ideas on chaotic systems in the 1880s based on his observation of the unusual behavior of three bodies under the influence of gravity as identified by Newton. Chaotic behavior was also investigated in the later part of the 19th century by Jacques Hadamard, another French mathematician, in the context of an object sliding on a frictionless surface. However, real progress was not made until such systems could be modeled using electronic computers.

The main problem in the observation of chaotic behavior is that patterns only emerge after thousands or even millions of iterations. It is extremely tedious to plot these patterns by hand. Computers on the other hand can be easily programmed to produce numerous iterations. Edward Lorenz discovered the power of input-sensitivity by accident using a computer program he had developed to predict weather patterns.[9] Lorenz noticed that the computer was producing different outcomes after thousands of iterations because the computer had a rounding error. Input sensitivity was the reason. Since then, all sorts of disciplines have been discovered to exhibit chaotic or nonlinear behavior such as weather theory, earth science, economics, biology, and information theory.

Chaos theory has forced scientists to dramatically alter the way they look at data and even the nature of reality. The Chaotic Thinker asks: what will happen if I vary the inputs just a wee bit and run the simulation for hundreds, thousands, or even millions of times? Will the pattern repeat or will a new pattern emerge? Novelists have popularized these questions with books, films, and series, such as "It's a Wonderful Life," "The Butterfly Effect," "Sliding Doors," or "Fringe." What if I miss that train? What if I commit suicide? What will the world look like? Will it be different? Will it be better or worse? The Chaotic Thinker is very aware of the power of variation in physical systems and the role of choice in human decision making. More on this concept later in the chapter.

The Relativistic Thinker

When you are courting a nice girl an hour seems like a second. When you sit on a red-hot cinder a second seems like an hour. That's relativity.

—Albert Einstein

No matter how hard you try to teach your cat general relativity, you're going to fail.

—Brian Greene, physicist

The Relativistic Thinker understands that anyone (i.e., any observer) making measurements of events does so in the context of his or her *frame of reference.* In this sense, all events and measurements are *relative* to the frame of reference that contains the observer. The observer could be speeding away at millions of miles per hour in a rocket ship or could just be walking the earth. Each is considered to be in a valid frame of reference. According to relativity, no one observer is located in an absolute frame of reference; that is, all frames of reference are relative to each other and within each frame measurements are consistent. To put it simply, the Relativistic Thinker understands that all measurements and events take place relative to something else.

Albert Einstein was the first to propose that frames of reference are important, that the laws of physics are the same in all frames of reference, and that light beams always travel at the same speed[10] in all frames of reference. These simple insights led Einstein to revolutionize our ways of thinking about time and space, running experiments and making measurements, the relationship between matter and energy, the variability of time and length, and many other physical principles. Einstein is considered one of the greatest thinkers of all time because he was able to use his *imagination* to discover the true nature of space and time. It took nearly 75 years for experimental physics to verify all of Einstein's deductions. His life story contains many lessons.

Einstein was born in 1879 in the town of Ulm, Germany. His father was a salesman and engineer. He matured slowly and had a speech disorder as a child. Einstein attended high schools in Switzerland and Germany and even failed an entrance exam to one of them. After graduating from high school, he spent 2 years trying to find a teaching position, but to no avail. With some help from a family friend, he was made an assistant patent examiner in the Swiss Patent Office in Bern, where he later obtained a permanent position in 1905 at the age of 26. The same year, he published four papers on the topics of Brownian motion, the photoelectric effect, special relativity, and the equivalence of matter and energy; that is, his famous equation: $E = mc^2$.

Einstein's work revolutionized our understanding of physics in many ways. He was able to show that Newton's laws were are subset of his own work and also provide a plausible explanation for gravity using his expanded notion of space–time, something Newton admitted he was unable to do. Einstein continued to work on his ideas at Princeton

University until his death in 1955. Interestingly, as great a mathematician and physicist as he was, he never embraced quantum physics, which emerged in the 1930s under the leadership of Niels Bohr. Quantum physics, which applies to the subatomic realm of particles, makes many assumptions (see next section) that Einstein recoiled from philosophically. Quantum physics relies on statistical probabilities of events taking place in the subatomic world. Einstein was very uncomfortable with this idea, causing him to quip "God does not play dice with the universe." He believed, like the Determinists, that the universe is governed by laws not probabilities. As nimble as he was in his early years, he was unable to shift his ideas in this regard despite the fact that all the predictions of quantum physics were verified experimentally throughout the 20th century. In this sense, Einstein's life is a cautionary tale for those who embrace creative thinking. Sometimes we can become trapped by the blinders we adopt to contain our imagination.

In summary, the Relativistic Thinker understands that the perspective of the observer (and in particular, the location and speed of the observer) is important. Each observer looks at and measures the world relative to his or her frame of reference using the same tools and laws of physics. There are no absolute frames of reference and no center points in the universe. In this sense, all observers are equals. Philosophically, relativity teaches us humility.

The Quantum Thinker

If anybody says he can think about quantum physics without getting giddy, that only shows he has not understood the first thing about them.
—Niels Bohr. Danish Physicist, Nobel Prize for
Physics in 1922. 1885–1962

If quantum mechanics hasn't profoundly shocked you, you haven't understood it yet.

—Niels Bohr

The more success the quantum theory has, the sillier it looks.
—Albert Einstein. German-born American Physicist.
Nobel Prize for Physics in 1921. 1879–1955

If only the universe was as tidy as we would like it to be. The Quantum Thinker sees a very different world than the rest of us. The Quantum Thinker tolerates all sorts of ambiguity, contradiction, and bizarre behavior. Our common-sense notions of causality, differentiation, time, certainty, and conducting an experiment all are challenged at the quantum level. The Quantum Thinker must give up mental models that are so effective in dealing with our everyday world and truly embrace the bizarre events that occur in the quantum world. Why? Because every experiment ever conducted since its inception has validated all the fantastic claims of quantum physics. In the end, we are forced to accept reality *as it is* even if it makes us uncomfortable.

To clarify. The quantum level is defined as the distances between the constituents of atoms. Atoms are made up of electrons, protons, and neutrons. You may recall from grade school that atoms are depicted as mini-solar systems, where the electrons circle the nucleus composed of neutrons and protons. While useful, this picture of the atom is highly inaccurate. We now know that electrons cannot be located accurately, but exist in a sort of *probability-density cloud* somewhere around the nucleus. We also know that protons and neutrons are made up of all sorts of smaller components including quarks. Experiments on atoms are usually conducted by smashing them together at very high speeds in particle accelerators found at Lawrence Livermore or CERN. Scientists study the results of those interactions.

As we peered deeper and deeper into the atom in the early part of the 20th century, scientists were confronted with very confusing experimental data. So confusing that it led to a revolutionary new way of thinking about the world, one that even Albert Einstein had trouble accepting. Here are some of the tenants of Quantum Theory (see Table 6.3).

Quantum physics makes many, many crazy predictions, but after rigorous scientific testing, the predictions are always right! The truth, as strange as it may seem, is inescapable. Electrons do jump from one "orbit" to another, but only at a specific level of energy and not before. If we measure the speed of an electron, we are unable to locate it and vice versa. If we measure its location we have no idea how fast it was going. The problem is that the act of measuring changes the outcome of the experiment. Observers *do* affect the outcome of the experiment and the design

Table 6.3. Principle Tenants of Quantum Theory

Principle	Description
Quantization	• Electrons "jump" from one state to another with no state in between
Uncertainty	• We cannot know the exact location and speed of electrons, only probabilities
Duality	• Particles and light can exhibit both wave and particle-like behaviors
Multiple worlds	• Setting up the experiment *can* determine the behavior we see • At every given instant, all possible states can occur
Entanglement	• Two particles can be entangled in such a way that changes in one can result in instantaneous changes in the other regardless of distance
Superposition	• One particle can be in superposition to itself; that is, it can appear as a wave of potential and can interfere with itself to create an interference pattern
Role of the observer	• The observer is always part of the measurement system • Observers can *change* the outcomes of events

of an experiment can affect what we see. It was also shown mathematically that all possible events can occur in a single experiment.

The most famous example of this occurs in the double slit experiment where a single electron is shot at a screen with two double slits in it (Figure 6.1). It can be proven that the electron goes through *the left*

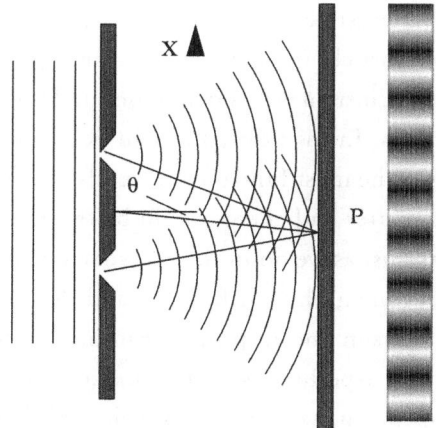

Figure 6.1 The double slit experiment[11]

or right slit, no slits or both slits and every other permutation in the same experiment. It makes no sense but it is reality at the quantum level. But there is more. Scientists found that two particles can be entangled such that changes in one produce changes in the other, even at great distances. Particles can interfere with themselves; that is, they can somehow participate in multiple events in the same experiment and their waves patterns interfere with each other. Uncertainty is the rule. Finally, quantum physics draws attention to role of the observer. The observer has an impact on the outcome of an experiment. Scientists found that when they positioned detectors near events, the outcomes of those experiments changed. We don't know why this is true, but it is true nonetheless. The notions of the independent observer and the cool detachment of scientific experiments were challenged by these findings.

To sell this vision of the world to the rest of the scientific community was no small feat. Niels Bohr was the leader of this movement in the 1930s. Bohr was born in Copenhagen, Denmark in 1885. His father was professor of physiology at the University of Copenhagen, and his mother came from a family involved in banking and politics. Bohr also became a professor at the University of Copenhagen in 1916 in theoretical physics. He was awarded the Nobel Prize for his contributions to the understanding of subatomic particles. His interpretation of the experimental data was this: At the most fundamental level of matter and energy, there is no causality or deterministic cause for events. He argues that they "just happen" with certain probabilities. Furthermore, it is possible that an object (e.g., an electron) can be both a wave and particle (or both at the same time) depending on how we measure it. Einstein was very opposed and uncomfortable with these interpretations. In his heart, Einstein believed in determinism. He believed that at the most fundamental levels of space and time that events involving matter and energy could be traced back to causes or initial conditions, just as we do in the everyday world by applying the principles of Newtonian physics. Einstein and Bohr staged a series of debates, both in person and in print, regarding the interpretation of data emerging from experiments at the subatomic level. Despite Einstein's best arguments, he was unable to shake Bohr's interpretation of the results. By the late 1930s, Bohr's interpretation of quantum physics (e.g., "The Copenhagen Interpretation") was generally accepted by the scientific community; Einstein had lost. Since then, several alternative interpretations of quantum have been proposed,[12] but they share most of the essential elements of Bohr's assessment. Bohr's leadership, and tenacity, changed the mental models of the greatest minds in physics and helped usher in the next revolution in solid-state electronics and innovations.

In summary, the Quantum Thinker tolerates ambiguity and uncertainty (like the Statistical Thinker or the Nonlinear Thinker). He or she accepts the outcomes of experiments and scientific testing despite the fact the results may contradict what we know about the world from common sense and every-day experience. He or she does not cling stubbornly to fantasies about the way the world *should* be, but accepts *how it is*. This acceptance requires a certain level of maturity. The Quantum Thinker is very aware of the role of the observer in shaping the outcome of the experiment, as well as the impact of the design on what is observed. Furthermore, he or she is able to tolerate the underlying mystery that events involving particles at the subatomic level can just occur with certain probabilities without a priori causes. The Quantum Thinker is both scientist and mystic at heart.

Summary of the Scientific Thinkers

In this chapter, we have covered six different types of thinkers as can be seen in Table 6.4. Each thinker has a distinctive profile (as outlined earlier) and a distinct focus. For example, the Intuitive Thinker sees the world in common-sense terms. In contrast, the Deterministic Thinker looks for rules, regularities, and causes. The Quantum Thinker lives in a strange world that runs counter to common sense. He or she must tolerate great ambiguity, conflicting data, and conclusions that just may seem crazy.

Each way of thinking embodies a certain philosophy of the world and relies on certain mental models. It is important to identify which thinker you are most closely aligned with currently, as well as considering which ones you may embrace in the future.

Table 6.4 Types of thinkers

Thinker type	Primary focus	Core beliefs
The Intuitive Thinker	Common-sense notions from our everyday experience	Belief that common sense and everyday experience are sufficient to understand the world
The Deterministic Thinker	Laws, rules, and equations. The inevitability of certain outcomes	Belief that the world can be reduced to laws, rules, and causality
The Stochastic Thinker	Role of chance and randomness. Large data sets and central tendency to the mean	Belief that we can predict the future from historical data Belief that random variation is to be expected
The Chaotic Thinker	Input-sensitivity. Nonlinear behavior. "Butterfly Effect"	Belief that an individual (small input) can change the system
The Relativistic Thinker	Everything is defined relative to a frame of reference. Observer's frame of reference important	Belief that each observer's comes from a unique frame of reference Belief that there are multiple points of view
The Quantum Thinker	Counter intuitive propositions about time, space, and events. Role of the observer	Belief that an observer can affect the outcome of an event Belief that in every instant the choices we make can lead to different "realities"

Relationship Between Scientific Modes of Thinking and Creativity

What is the relationship between the philosophical foundations of each thinker and creative expression? These models of reality exert a powerful influence on how you view the world and your capacity to take action, effect change, and to express your creative impulses. In my opinion, some views are more conducive to creative thought than others.

The Chaotic Thinker, the Relativistic Thinker, and the Quantum Thinker all have views that support creative expression. The Chaotic thinker fosters the belief that small changes can produce large outcomes. Each of us represents the potential to make small changes to the system, be an organization, a community, a state, a country, or even the world. The Chaotic Thinker encourages us to exercise our creativity and to effect change locally with the understanding that it may result in changes on a larger scale. The Relativistic Thinker understands that there are multiple points of view and that every observer has a unique frame of reference. Although this idea was applied originally by Einstein to moving inertial frames of reference, it translates well into world of aesthetics and social interaction. The Quantum Thinker brings the unique notion that our choices, in every single instant, make a difference to how the world evolves. Furthermore, the Quantum Thinker understands the role of the observer in the act of observation. Observers can impact the outcome of experiments.

On the other hand, the Deterministic Thinker has beliefs that most run counter to creative expression. The belief in a universe governed by laws that produce predictable outcomes does not allow for human free will and creative expression. Similarly, the Statistical Thinker by focusing on the law of large numbers cannot account for the behavior of a single individual, like a Gandhi or a Gorbchev, who have the capacity to dramatically change the state of the system. Finally, the Intuitive Thinker looks at the world in everyday terms and so much of creative expression is grounded in realism. On the other hand, there are times when we need to look at the world from alternative views, be they abstract, impressionist, or avant-garde. In the next section, we examine the role of experimentation as a means to test scientific theories.

Experimentation Is the Cornerstone of the Scientific Method

The primary factor that distinguishes science from mathematics is that scientific theories must be tested via *experiments*. This process is what defines the scientific method. The components of this process are illustrated in Figure 6.2. As can be seen, the process begins with the framing of a hypothesis based on a scientific worldview. Next, the researcher frames an experiment to collect data about the object or event being investigated. Once analyzed, the results are used to either refine the model or to reject it. This cycle of *theory–test–revise* remains ongoing for years, even centuries, until a theory is considered bulletproof or it is discarded.

Experimentation is therefore the cornerstone of scientific discovery. Experimentation begins with the *design* and implementation of an

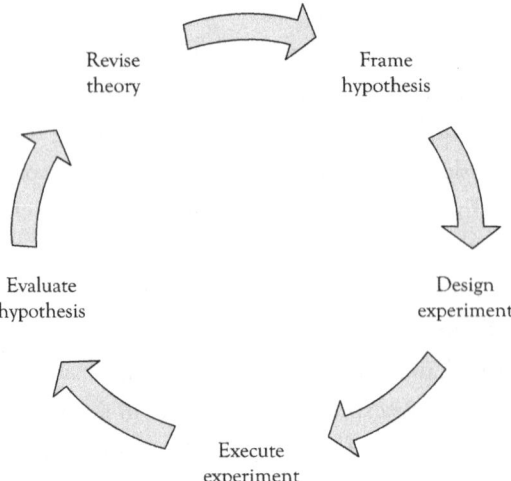

Figure 6.2 The process for testing scientific theories

experiment. The experiment itself is an opportunity to *observe* an event or object under certain conditions built into the design.[13] Both start with an in-depth connection between an observer and some object or process. Scientists collect sensory input (i.e., data) to test certain hypotheses and assumptions. Once the data is collected, it is analyzed for patterns and regularities. The next step is to *invent* a model that helps to explain the data that has been collected.

Notice the words used above. *Design. Observation. Invention.* The scientific method (and experimentation) is a highly creative activity bounded only by our imagination and the constraints imposed by the physical world. It shares many of the attributes of art, music, and architecture and is a process of innovation.

Here is the working definition of experimentation that we shall use throughout this book:

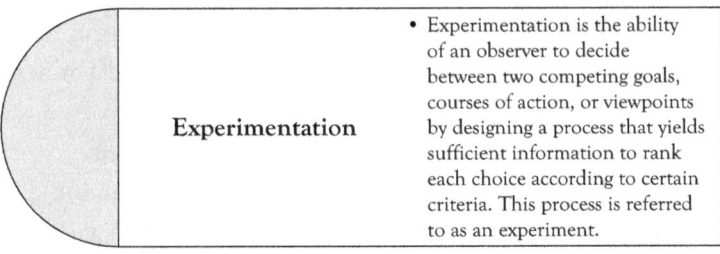

Experimentation

- Experimentation is the ability of an observer to decide between two competing goals, courses of action, or viewpoints by designing a process that yields sufficient information to rank each choice according to certain criteria. This process is referred to as an experiment.

The Importance and Role of Tinkering

It is important to point out that experimentation exists on a continuum in terms of being a highly structured to a loosely structured activity. Formal experiments are conducted by large organizations such as CERN, the National Institutes of Health, large pharmaceutical companies and large research-oriented universities. In these instances, the process is highly structured and rigorous and adheres to well-documented rules and policies that govern research. However, all organizations, large and small, can conduct experiments using scientific methods by framing hypotheses, designing and running experiments, and examining the results. Money does not have to be an issue. An organization can thus test the implementation of a new product design or the look and feel of a new website using scientific methods at modest expense.

Individuals can do the same. We can design experiments to help us make a variety of decisions from which jeans are more durable to the best format for a resume to the relative merits of advertising a new business idea using Google AdWords versus Facebook. The experiment itself can be much less structured and more aptly characterized as *tinkering*. Tinkering amounts to changing and modifying something in an exploratory way; that is, as a means to produce knowledge and understanding, but also to simply learn[14] (see Figure 6.3). Children are especially good at tinkering because they are naturally curious.[15] Adults, on the other hand, typically are not so practiced at tinkering. This is an important skill to add to your repertoire and one that can be engaged in at any time.

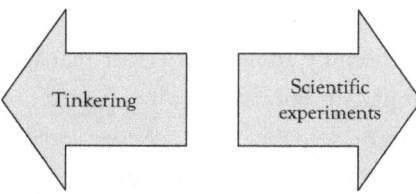

Figure 6.3 The continuum of tinkering and scientific experimentation

Develop Your Experimental Mind and Skills

Prepare

To begin, familiarize yourself with the various schools of thought as outlined in this chapter. Next, understand the scientific method and the methods of experimentation. Do a Google search on "scientific methods," "experimentation," and "tinkering" to find documents and videos on the topics. You are also encouraged to take a science class to learn the fundamentals or to mentor with a scientist.

Practice

It is useful to explore the world by creating opportunities to learn in action. *Action learning* is an educational process by which individuals or groups of people learn through practice. It can be a very loosely structured process along the lines of "tinkering," or can be more structured where we have specific goals that we wish to achieve. For example, imagine you and your spouse always fight over who does the dishes. Imagine other responses you might have to the situation and act on them. What did you learn? Another example. Consider what you will do if you encounter a wait-person who is rude. Write down several responses; for example, getting angry, asking the person what is wrong, being super-nice, remaining silent, asking to see the manager, and so forth. The next time you are in that situation you can learn about yourself through the actions you take. An essential aspect of action learning, therefore, is to reflect on the results of your actions. As you do, you will be modifying your mental models about yourself and others. In short, you will learn. The next step is to incorporate action learning into your professional and personal life.

Perform

These ideas can be usefully applied for career management, hobbies, or for personal development. For example, if you are a hobbyist farmer, you can run experiments on seed types (e.g., conventional vs. organic), watering methods, or plant density. Similarly, you can apply tinkering to the structure of your resume or how to communicate with colleagues. When you approach life with an experimental attitude, you become a *reflective practitioner*.[16]

Chapter Summary

Science provides many lessons for the aspiring artist, creator, or designer. Discovering the secrets of nature is an exercise in structured imagination. The history of science is populated with people who have exercised their imagination to construct mental models of the physical world. These models exert a powerful influence on the way we think and especially in the way we design. Designs are built out of images and values and so constrain our imagination. If you live in a universe governed by laws and rules, and controlled in by distant forces, you are likely to build organizations and artifacts similarly constructed. If you live in a universe of choice and random fluctuations, your designs will evolve differently. The history of science is a lesson in the power of models and of structured imagination. It is the discipline of testing what we imagine that is the cornerstone of experimentation. We imagine the way the world is, set up conditions to test those assumptions, and record the results. Sometimes we are surprised with the results as was the case in the world of quantum physics. Other times, the results only strengthen our beliefs in the dominant paradigm. In either case, the experiments we run lead to new knowledge about the world we inhabit and the potential world we can design.

CHAPTER 7

Deepen Your Aesthetic Awareness

Leonardo da Vinci combined art and science and aesthetics and engineering; that kind of unity is needed once again.
—Ben Shneiderman, Professor of Computer
Human Interaction

The word aesthetics is one that is seldom used in the context of business. We usually talk about the bottom line, profits, or business models, but let me convince you that aesthetics is just as important. Aesthetics is one of the primary means for evaluating creations (from the viewpoint of the consumer), and it is a fundamental component of design (from the viewpoint of the designer). Although it may be assumed to be restricted to the judgment of works of art, don't be fooled; every consumer is evaluating products and services based on aesthetic measures. Failure to recognize this insight can lead to economic peril for an organization.

Furthermore, the knowledge that results from the information that comes to us through our senses is just as important as knowledge that arises from logical–rational analysis. Indeed, the ability to perceive and make aesthetic judgments is a strength just as important as learning how to design, improvise or to your leverage your multiple intelligences.

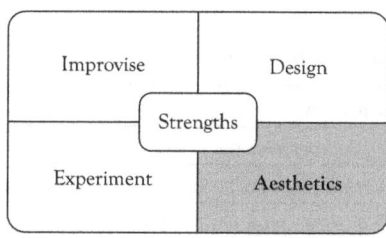

Defining Aesthetics

The concept of aesthetics has a long history. Aesthetics finds its roots in the Greek words, *aisthetikos*, which means "sensitive, perceptive," and *aisthanesthai*, which means, "to perceive (by the senses or by the mind), to feel."[1]

The great German philosopher Immanuel Kant used aesthetics to describe the conditions under which human beings are engaged in perception of the world around them through their senses. His contribution to our understanding of aesthetics appears in his *Critique of Judgment* published in 1790.[2] Kant distinguished between two types of sensory experiences: pure and impure. Interactions between the observer and nature were considered "pure," whereas interactions with human-made or designed objects (such as art) were considered "impure."

In the context of art, the aesthetic is commonly defined as that which gives or is designed to give pleasure through the sensation of beauty.[3] However, aesthetics does not have to be restricted in scope to the appreciation of art alone. Such evaluations can be made with regard to any object or process.

The Aesthetic Process

The steps that occur in the interaction between an observer and an object of aesthetic judgment can be summarized as follows (see Table 7.1).

The aesthetic process begins with pure sensory recording. What is my perception of the object? Next (even before thought), we experience an emotion ranging from happy, to sad, disgusted, afraid, or angry. Thoughts and concepts then emerge in relation to our perception and

Table 7.1 The aesthetic process

Process	Function
Perception	How do I perceive the object?
Emotion	What emotions are generated in me as a result of this perception?
Thought	What thoughts occur as a result of this perception?
Evaluation	How would I evaluate this object in terms of beauty?

emotion. "What a lovely sunset," "How dreary and depressing this room is." Finally, we assign a value along a continuum in terms of the degree of beauty apparent in the object. All of this occurs in the blink of an eye and once our impressions are formed, it is difficult to undo, lending credence to the old saying, "Always make a good first impression because you will never get a second chance." Imagine if this is you or your product or service?

Developing aesthetic awareness is therefore another key skill for success in the 21st century. Here is the working definition of aesthetic awareness that we shall use in this book:

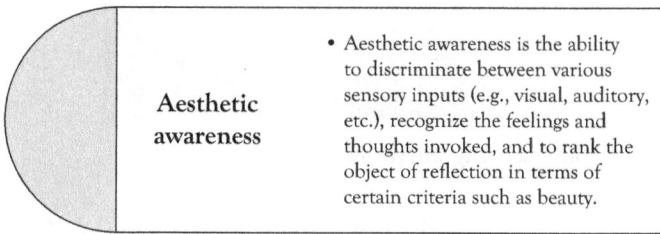

Aesthetic awareness

- Aesthetic awareness is the ability to discriminate between various sensory inputs (e.g., visual, auditory, etc.), recognize the feelings and thoughts invoked, and to rank the object of reflection in terms of certain criteria such as beauty.

Aesthetic Experiences as Sensory Experiments

We can think of an aesthetic experience as a sort of sensory experiment. When we set up a scientific experiment, we have a few essential elements: an observer, an object or event for observation, and a set of observations. The outcome of the experiment is a description of the event and some sort of explanation or model of the results.

In an aesthetic context, there is also an observer and an object or event for observation (see for example Figure 7.1). However, the outcome of an aesthetic experiment is a complex cognitive and emotional reaction to the sensory data. The "experiment" may produce happiness, sadness, revulsion, or some other emotion. Accompanying that emotion will be a set of ideas and judgments that position the object or the experience on a scale of beauty. The object may be judged to be beautiful or ugly or somewhere in between. Every time we encounter a new structure, product, or service, we engage in a sensory experiment. The result of each of these "experiments" strengthens or weakens the mental models we have constructed based on previous encounters with similar artifacts.

Figure 7.1 Baby kissing mirror image[4]

Applying Aesthetics to Organizational Life

The concept of aesthetics has also worked its way into the narrative on modern organizational life. "Aesthetics in organizational life 'concerns … (a) the knowledge yielded by the perceptive faculties of hearing, sight, touch, smell, and taste and (b) by the capacity for aesthetic judgment.' "[5] A firm can be beautiful or it can be ugly. Products can be beautiful or ugly.

The aesthetic experience can be one of total immersion between the observer and the object of evaluation. "The aesthetic can be defined as the simultaneous, and unified, engagement of the mind, body, and sensibilities."[6] What is striking about this definition is the total connectedness between observer and the object of observation. Imagine if this is the connection between you and your products or services, or place of work. Aesthetics informs what we see, hear, and touch, what we feel, and our judgment of the object.

We apply aesthetic judgments to products, services, or to the workplace itself. For example, here is an assessment of the aesthetics of the quality of an organization's sensory environment illustrated in Table 7.2.

While the physical layout and design of your workplace is not the sole determining factor of quality of work life, it certainly is a contributing

Table 7.2 The aesthetic process applied to a workplace environment

Process	Function
Perception	How do I perceive my workplace? (i.e., the buildings, the workspaces, etc.)
Emotion	What emotions are generated in me as I perceive my workplace?
Thought	What thoughts occur as a result of this perception?
Evaluation	How would I evaluate my workplace environment in terms of beauty?

Table 7.3 Workplace environments[7]

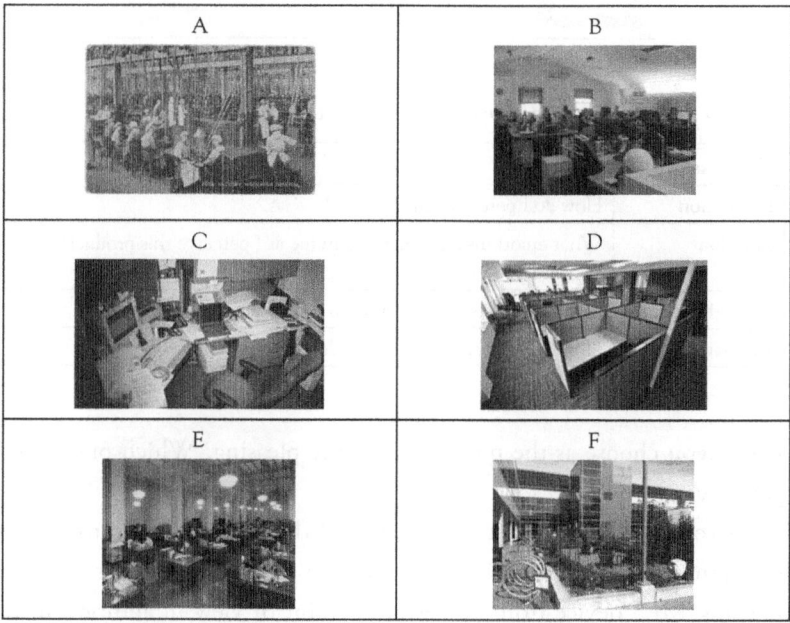

factor. Ask any working person how they perceive their workplace and you will get an answer ranging from beautiful to ugly. Some people may feel depressed and other happy or inspired. Here, for example, are a few pictures of various workplace environments shown in Table 7.3. How would you evaluate these workplaces in terms of aesthetics? Which one would you prefer to work in?

Applying Aesthetics to Product Design and Evaluation

The same type of evaluation process can be applied to products or services. Let's look at four MP3 players shown in Table 7.4. Which one

Table 7.4 Visual comparisons of MP3 players[8]

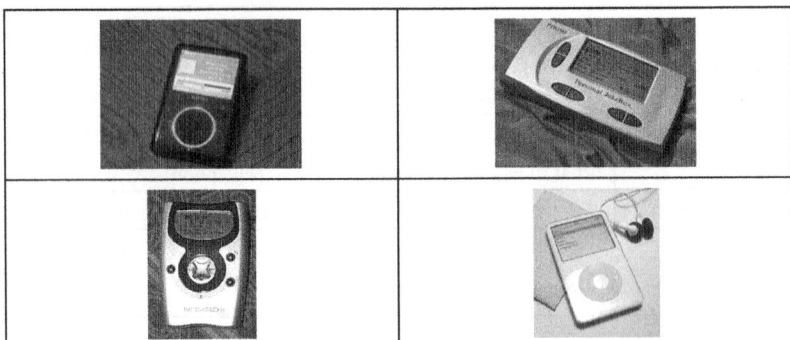

Table 7.5 The aesthetic process applied to products

Process	Function
Perception	How do I perceive this product?
Emotion	What emotions are generated in me as I perceive this product and imagine using it?
Thought	What thoughts occur as a result of this perception?
Evaluation	How would I evaluate this product in terms of beauty?

would you choose as the most aesthetically pleasing? Which one would you buy?

If you are like most people you picked the iPod in the bottom right quadrant as the most beautiful and desirable. Why? Because it is the most pleasing MP3 device from an aesthetic point of view in addition to its great functionality. The process is the same as shown in Table 7.5. Form and function matter when it comes to purchasing decisions. Aesthetics is fundamental to good design, although it is not the whole story. Good design includes consideration for economics, usability, and manufacturability in addition to aesthetics.[9]

Services can be similarly measured in terms of the quality of the interactions between the client and your people. Did the employee have a beautiful personality, face, smile, clothes, and so forth? What was the tone of his or her voice? Was it beautiful or ugly? What was the attitude like? All of these factors play into the client's evaluation of your service and your company and whether or not they will purchase your services in the future.

Consequences of Aesthetic Awareness and Engagement

What are some of the likely consequences of adopting an aesthetic perspective? For individuals, aesthetic experiences sharpen our sense of perception. We really start to look at the artifacts around us, which makes us discerning observers of the lives that we lead and the contexts in which we are embedded. Once we see, we also connect with the emotions that are automatically generated within us as a consequence of our sight. Do these things make us happy or sad? As we cultivate our aesthetic awareness, we also become better-educated consumers of everything, from art to cars to iPods to entertainment. We come to appreciate the elements of good design and demand more from those who supply us with goods and services.

By conducting aesthetic evaluations, we sharpen our abilities to perceive, feel, and conceptualize and to evaluate. More importantly, aesthetic awareness cultivates a state of being much like mindfulness or flow. By fully engaging the mind, body, and sensibilities,[10] we are more connected and energized. That outcome in turn affects other people with who we interact in ways foreseen and unforeseen.

In our work contexts, we become more effective as employees, managers, designers, and leaders. One could argue that a deeper appreciation of the aesthetic dimensions of organizational life goes hand in hand with the objectives of human resource development.

> The discipline of HRD could in fact be defined as ... concerned precisely with the theory and practice of engaging simultaneously the mind, body, and sensibilities, in the course of developing people and organizations. The same set of concerns that are found in aesthetics exist and live in HRD.[11]

Thus, the goal of human resource development is to develop employees to attain a state of aesthetic immersion. I couldn't agree more. Cultivating employees who are perceptive of the world around them and fully engaged in both mind and body is the goal of any leader. Leadership has always been considered an "art" for this reason.

Furthermore, leaders and mentors help to develop and enrich follower's, not only by helping them to apprehend functional and "how-to"

Table 7.6 Summary of outcomes of aesthetic awareness for individuals

Attributes
• Heightened ability to see and perceive
• Ability to evaluate works of art as well as products, services
• Recognition of flow and focus (mindfulness) as aspects of everyday life, including work life
• Belief that art permeates all of life including the workplace
• Results in the infusion of energy to our lives and the social contexts that we inhabit
• Can lead to improved quality of work life

knowledge, but also the "knowledge yielded by the perceptive faculties of hearing, sight, touch, smell and taste, and ... the capacity for aesthetic judgment."[12]

Finally, embracing the aesthetic dimension generates energy. When we are engaged, we are energized. Aesthetics cultivates a state similar to flow described in a previous chapter. In flow, as in this aesthetic state of engagement, we are energized yet relaxed at the same time. Time becomes irrelevant. We are connected to the object of our attention. Our emotional state is one of well being and positive affect. We experience this energy as individuals, which can flow into our teams and our organizations. These individual outcomes are summarized in Table 7.6. The social implications of aesthetics are described in more detail in *"Designing Creative High Power Teams and Organizations: Beyond Leadership,"* also available from Business Expert Press. For now, focus on developing your own aesthetic awareness at home, work and other social contexts.

Developing Aesthetic Awareness

Prepare

Developing aesthetic awareness begins with the premise that the information that comes to you through your senses (i.e., sight, hearing, taste, smell, and touch) and the resulting knowledge (i.e., thoughts, emotions, and evaluations) are as important to your success in organizational (and other) contexts as your knowledge of goals, tasks, and structures. Aesthetic awareness is strength just as important as interpersonal or mathematical intelligence and time should be devoted to its development.

Practice

There are many ways to practice. Certainly you can go to a museum to look at art, but that is just a starting point. Exercise aesthetic judgments in all aspects of your life and take note of the outcomes. Keep a journal. Record your thoughts, feelings, and evaluations. A digital camera is an excellent tool to develop perception and aesthetic awareness. Take picture of your home or outdoors. Even an object as simple as a ball can become the focal point for a series of photos that can lead to greater aesthetic awareness.

Perform

Take a really good look at your workplace and take pictures of it. Is it beautiful or ugly? Why? How about your products or services? How would you evaluate them? Organize a group to evaluate the aesthetic dimensions of your products or services. What are the results? Perhaps after doing so, you will have a much better understanding of what your customers think of your firm's creations.

Chapter Summary

Aesthetics is a critical but oftentimes overlooked component of competitive advantage. Aesthetics is about perception. Yours. Mine. Your customer's. Good design depends on aesthetic forms as well as carefully thought-out functionality. Buyers instinctively know what they like even if they can't express it. Recall that the aesthetic process is one of *Perception–Emotion–Thought–Evaluation*. Every time a person perceives a new artifact, they associate feelings with that sensory input. Happy, sad, or indifferent feelings precede any thoughts or evaluations that result. The look and feel of an object can confer power, pleasure, or energy. Alternatively, it can evoke indifference, dislike, or other negative feelings. Every interaction is thus a sensory experiment between the designer and the observer (or consumer) as mediated by the object of creation. In work contexts, the forms that surround us either enliven us depress us. They add energy or take energy away. It is, therefore, important to consider the physical environment as an important component of organizational design, which is described in more detail in "*Designing Creative High Power Teams and Organizations: Beyond Leadership*," also available from Business Expert Press.

CHAPTER 8

A Plan for Action

No great thing is created suddenly.
        —Epictetus—Greek philosopher, Stoics, AD 55–c.135

The purpose of this final chapter is to tie together the lessons learned from the previous chapters. It is designed to help you to maximize the potential offered by your strengths and to master four new skills: improvisation, design thinking, experimentation, and aesthetic awareness. In short, my goal is to provide you with a plan of action for development and transformation.

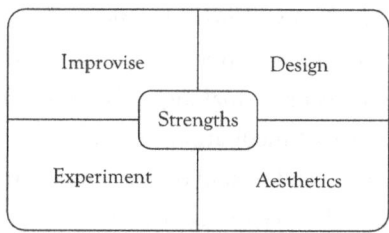

Step 1: Inventory Your Thoughts and Cognitions

The biggest lesson I have ever learned is the stupendous importance of what we think. If I knew what you think, I would know what you are, for your thoughts make you what you are; by changing our thoughts, we can change our lives.
        —Dale Carnegie, motivational speaker

This book began by shining a spotlight on your dominant assumptions and *theories in use*[1] that you have about yourself and others. *Theories in use* arise from our observations of the world as we learn and discern relationship between causes and effects. Sets of these *theories in use* (e.g., about work, relationships, etc.) result in the formation of *mental models* and behaviors that help us to navigate through life. Some are more functional than others. Taken as a whole, your mental models result in what is referred to as your *worldview*.

The key to reaching your creative potential is first to take an inventory of your assumptions, mental models, and patterns of thought. The language we use is indicative of our underlying assumptions. Paying attention to the words, analogies, and images we use is critical. Using *dichotomies*, framing *universal statements*, or resorting to *Us versus Them* thinking delays or impedes your ability to create. The first step therefore is to recognize that you may be falling into these traps.

Step 2: Realign Your Cognitions and Behaviors

Once you become aware of the language you use and the accompanying thought patterns, you need to challenge the negative thoughts and cultivate new patterns of thinking and behaviors to prepare yourself for the experience of creating. You will first become aware of the voice of judgment and other dysfunctional patterns of thought. Meet these head on by refuting these judgments or by making them look ridiculous as noted in Chapter 2. The practice of meditation can make you aware of the many voices in your head that tend to stall or prevent creative thinking and will sharpen your senses and perceptions. Meditation can also lead to *flow* as experienced by designers, artists, and musicians. Both meditation and the practice of artistic pursuits result in *mindfulness*; that is, being connected and immersed in the present moment. Immersion in these and other reflective activities can help you to cultivate the *beginner's mind*. Engage your curiosity.

Step 3: Leverage Your Strengths

The next step in the process is to take stock of and leverage your innate strengths. Use Howard Gardner's theory of multiple intelligences as a guide. Assess your relative strengths in the eight categories he specifies as noted in Chapter 3: verbal–linguistic intelligence; mathematical–logical intelligence; musical intelligence; visual–spatial intelligence; bodily kinesthetic intelligence; interpersonal intelligence; intrapersonal intelligence;

and naturalist intelligence. Make sure you really understand these eight areas of strength. Reading about extraordinary people in each category is useful. Once you have used an online assessment tool to construct your multiple intelligence profile, take some time to reflect on whether these represent areas of strength *you have chosen* or were *chosen by other people*. You now have the option to choose. Consider too your strategy: Do you want to build on existing strengths or to focus on ones that require development? This is a critical choice. It is also important to look at your top two or three strengths relative to each other. Can you leverage these combinations to pursue a new job or career? Unusual combinations can provide you with a competitive advantage over others in the marketplace.

Step 4: Add New Skills to Your Repertoire

In addition to expanding your natural strengths and abilities, all 21st-century professionals should add these four essential creative skills to their repertoire: improvisation, design thinking, experimentation, and aesthetic awareness (see Table 8.1).

Epictetus said, "No great thing is created suddenly," and so it is with attaining mastery of these skills. To reach the level of master (and beyond) will require 10,000 hours. I, suggest that you employ the P3 method to cultivate attainment of each skill: Prepare, Practice, and Perform.

Table 8.1 Definitions of new skills

Area	Definition
Improvisation	*Improvisation* is the ability to make effective real-time decisions in new and complex situations using current information and appropriately chosen (or modified) routines, scripts, and patterns
Design	*Design* is the ability to envision and construct an object or a process that meets the goals and requirements of a particular user
Experimentation	*Experimentation* is the ability of an observer to decide between two competing goals, courses of action, or viewpoints by designing a process that yields sufficient information to rank each choice according to certain criteria. This process is often referred to as an experiment
Aesthetic awareness	*Aesthetic awareness* is the ability to discriminate between various sensory inputs (e.g., visual, auditory, etc.), recognize the feelings and thoughts invoked, and to rank the object of reflection in terms of certain criteria such as beauty

Preparation

Preparation typically means studying the rudiments of the domain through books, articles, websites, and so forth. It is also useful to conduct informational interviews with designers, improvisers, scientists, and artists in several fields to really understand the essence of what they do. All industries from energy to pharmaceuticals to automobiles, to space travel are built on scientific principles, and there will be no shortage of people to interview about experimentation and the scientific method. Talk to artists, art critics, and designers to learn how they employ aesthetic principles to make design choices. Interview product designers and architects to learn about their decision-making processes and methods. Interview musicians, comedians, and dancers of all stripes to get a better understanding of performance and improvisation. Most people hold very limited views of what creative people actually do and find the experience eye-opening.

Practice

Practice typically involves engaging in small projects that are designed to maximize learning rather than production. For example, to learn to improvise on a musical instrument, attend a jazz workshop or go to a jam session. Most experienced improvisers will welcome you and provide a supportive environment in which to test your abilities. In my own case, in addition to lessons and self-study, I have attended numerous immersive jazz workshops throughout the United States.[2] Not only did I learn about "chords" and "harmonies," but also learned about my own tolerance for risk, about self-doubt and self-imposed judgments, about ways to learn new and oftentimes difficult material, and how to work together with others in improvisational teams. I met many incredible people at these conferences, and I encourage you to participate in activities like this; you will not be disappointed.

There are many opportunities to practice design thinking. Build with Legos, develop a smart phone application, design clothes in Second Life, or build virtual communities using programs such as SimCity. At its heart, design is about learning a language and applying it to the creation of new processes and artifacts. The photographer learns the vocabulary of colors and light. The composer learns the vocabulary of sounds. The architect learns the vocabulary of form, function, and materials, and is able to experiment using computer-aided design programs. Nonprofessionals too can learn the elements of design using Google's SketchUp or Adobe's Photoshop. Now more than ever there are numerous tools and programming languages that allow nonprofessionals to express their design instincts.

Experimentation can be practiced both formally and informally. Informally, you can "tinker" with aspects of your life and keep a journal in order to reflect and learn from the outcomes. For example, you might be experiencing gastric distress each day. Instead of simply popping a pill, keep a log of what you eat and analyze the results. Which foods resulted in more or less distress? Can you change your diet in any way?[3] You can tinker with just about any aspect of your life. Many ideas on tinkering can be found in Tim Ferriss's book on personal productivity,[4] from gazing at strangers to getting phone numbers to using the active voice to propose courses of action (e.g., "I suggest that we should do X" rather than ask, "What should we do?") to cold-calling famous people. He calls them *comfort challenges* because they take us out of our comfort zone. We can also tinker with how we interact with others by changing the inflection in our voice, our tone, or the words we choose. The important thing to remember is to reflect on what you learn in each instance.

Formal experimental methods are built from these same principles but with more time spent in the design of the experiment itself, attention paid to the rigor of the record keeping, and the level and complexity of the analysis. These skills are best acquired through formal training and educational environments. That being said, anyone can implement scientific methods in pursuit of hobbies or pastimes. For example, amateur astronomers have made many important discoveries of comets, stars, and other celestial objects throughout history. Many scientists from previous eras such as Ben Franklin wore several hats and learned to experiment on their own. Much more than a scientist, Franklin was an author, printer, political theorist, politician, postmaster, musician, inventor, satirist, civic activist, statesman, and diplomat. Despite his many interests, he was able to make credible contributions to the fields of electricity and optics. You can too.[5]

Finally, there are numerous opportunities to practice aesthetic awareness. Museums are the first obvious choice but there are many other means of exploring aesthetics. Travelling to a new city (especially in another country) exposes you to designs that may be fundamentally different than those that you are accustomed to. Different architects (especially those from different eras) used different materials and forms (i.e., *vocabulary*) to express their ideas about structures. Every new city thus provides an opportunity to engage in aesthetic awareness. Product trade shows or conferences that bring designers together are another means to experience the aesthetics of design. Photography is another excellent vehicle for observing the world around you, from natural landscapes, to consumer products, to industrial designs, to cityscapes. Cultivating aesthetic awareness unites with practicing mindfulness as noted earlier.

Performance

The final aspect of the P3 method is performance. Performance is about engaging in and sharing your new skill with others in a *social context*. The venue or context can be *personal* or *professional*.[6] The key here is the social aspect. It is one thing to practice a piano concerto by yourself; it is entirely another to perform it live for others to hear. A short personal story. On the final day of every jazz workshop I have ever attended, we perform one or two compositions that we practiced during the week. It is both scary and invigorating. Most of the time, my performance does not live up to my expectations. The fact that others (i.e., the audience) will hear me and judge me is frightening. Controlling your nerves is part of the process of becoming an accomplished performer and is what separates most amateurs from pros. It is important to find ways to perform your new skills in front of other people for it really to sink in and become part of you. Fortunately, the more you do it, the easier it becomes.

The Cycle of Action and Reflection

This process of personal development and transformation is cyclical (see Figure 8.1) and repeats itself over time. Each cycle is punctuated with periods of action and reflection.

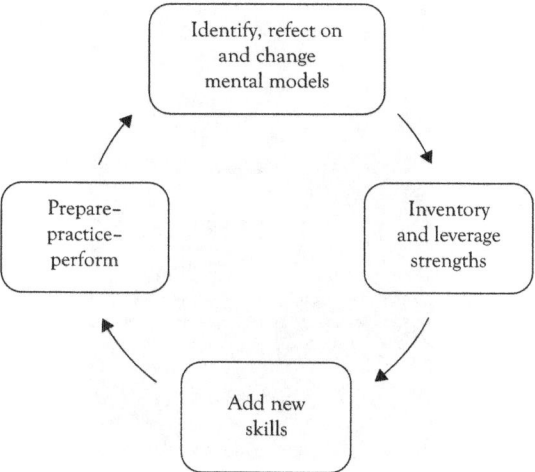

Figure 8.1 The transformational cycle of action and reflection

As you gain mastery of new skills and leverage strengths, you will change in subtle, yet important, ways. Throughout the cycle, you will confront many ideas about yourself and other people that can lead to *cognitive dissonance.*[7] This theory suggests that we experience psychological discomfort when we are confronted with two seemingly contradictory ideas, beliefs, values, or perceptions. Most people tend to address these feelings of discomfort by discarding one version of reality versus another in order to restore *consonance.* For instance, if your boss preached ethical behavior but was later caught for embezzlement, you would experience cognitive dissonance. Following a period of shock or denial, you would be forced to discard your old mental model of this person (i.e., "ethical person") in favor of a new one (i.e., hypocrite, liar, and cheat) based on the evidence. Similarly, the life of the creator is filled with such moments. It is expected that you will cycle through the processes of action and reflection many times throughout the journey, thus resulting in a *spiral* over time (see Figure 8.2). Reflecting in practice is therefore a necessary element of the journey.

A Note About Values and Closing Thoughts

Creative transformation is a human process, and I think it is important to close by highlighting the human aspects of this process. Fundamentally,

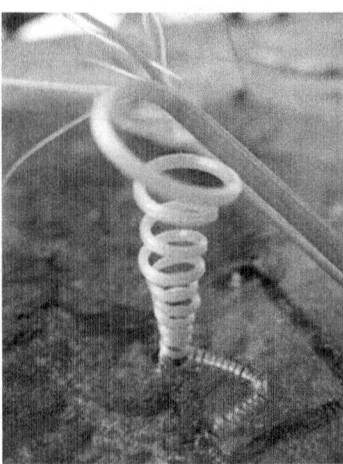

Figure 8.2 Illustration of the spiral of growth and transformation[8]

personal development is about making choices and expressing *values*. I am reminded of what the late Steve Jobs said in his commencement address to the graduates of Stanford University in 2005.[9] He left them with three important points: *connect the dots, love what you do*, and *make the most of the time you have*. His first point is about the power of reflection, a theme common to this book. In his words:

> Again, you can't connect the dots looking forward; you can only connect them looking backwards. So you have to trust that the dots will somehow connect in your future. You have to trust in some-thing— your gut, destiny, life, karma, whatever. This approach has never let me down, and it has made all the difference in my life.

He was referring to how his study of fonts and scripts at Reed College, a seemingly impractical pursuit, led to the development of proportional siz-ing and artistic fonts for the Macintosh computer (and all computers for that matter). Although he did not know it at the time, in hindsight and through reflection, he was able to understand how important that activity was for his future. What is implied is this: You must trust that the things that you are drawn to *now* will have significance in the future. He argues that it is through reflection that we make these connections.

His second point is about doing what you love. Again in his words:

You've got to find what you love. And that is as true for your work as it is for your lovers. Your work is going to fill a large part of your life, and the only way to be truly satisfied is to do what you believe is great work. And the only way to do great work is to love what you do. If you haven't found it yet, keep looking. Don't settle. As with all matters of the heart, you'll know when you find it. And, like any great relationship, it just gets better and better as the years roll on. So keep looking until you find it. Don't settle.

Put another way: would you rather spend 10,000 hours doing something you love or otherwise? Take the time to identify your strengths and areas of interest. Commit to the ones to which you are most attracted and love.

His third point is about being authentic to yourself and using your time wisely. He illustrates this point with reference to his then recent diagnosis of pancreatic cancer. He said:

Your time is limited, so don't waste it living someone else's life. Don't be trapped by dogma—which is living with the results of other people's thinking. Don't let the noise of others' opinions drown out your own inner voice. And most important, have the courage to follow your heart and intuition. They somehow already know what you truly want to become. Everything else is secondary.

This quote I think gets to core of living a full and fulfilling life, one that is self-actualized. Make the most of your time. Be mindful. Be who you are. Trust yourself and your intuitions.

Finally, this journey is *social*; we do not live in isolation. This is one aspect of the path not addressed explicitly by Jobs. Patience is critical, which includes patience for yourself as well as others. In addition to trusting yourself, it is equally important to find people that you can trust and rely on. This is a consequence of living a life with integrity, commitment and respect for other people. A good friend of mine frequently repeated this quote, "We are all in the process of becoming."[10] It is not just about getting *there*. It is about being *here*. Embrace the journey as well as its fruits.

Appendix

I have put together a list of several resources classified by topic including books, articles, links, and multimedia (e.g., videos, audio, images, etc.).[1] Additional resources are also available at ideasmethod.com as well as from Business Expert Press.

Improvisation

Books and Papers	Nachmanovitch, S. (1991). *Free play: Improvisation in life and art.* New York, NY: Tarcher/Putnam.
	Hamilton, A. (2000). The art of improvisation and the aesthetics of imperfection. *British Journal of Aesthetics 40*(1), 168–185.
	Koppett, K. (2002). Business and the art of imperfection. *The British Journal of Administrative Management 33*(1), 26–27.
	McKnight, B., & Bontis, N. (2002). E-improvisation: Collaborative groupware technology expands the reach and effectiveness of organizational improvisation. *Knowledge and Process Management 9*(4), 219.
	Montuori, A. (2003). The complexity of improvisation and the improvisation of complexity: social science, art and creativity. *Human Relations 56*(2), 237–255.
	Stein, E. (2011). *Improvisation as model for real-time decision-making. Annals of Information Systems—Special Volume in Decision Support Systems: Supporting Real Time Decision-Making: The Role of Context in Decision Support on the Move* (Vol. 13, pp. 13–34). F. Burstein, P. Brezillon, and A. Zaslavsky.(Eds.). New York, NY: Springer.
	Zack, M. (2000). Jazz improvisation and organizing: once more from the top. *Organization Science 11*(2), 227–234.
Links	Jazz http://www.jazzreview.com/ http://www.pbs.org/jazz/

Multi-media	Jazz "Kind of Blue" album by Miles Davis on Columbia Records. 1959. "So What" (1958) featuring Miles Davis and John Coltrane, along with Wynton Kelly on piano, Jimmy Cobb on drums, and Paul Chambers on bass. Recorded at CBS Studies in NYC by producer Robert Herridge on April 2, 1959. From TED.com: Herbie Hancock | Profile on TED.com Herbie Hancock is an iconic jazz musician, known as much for his mastery of the traditional as he is for entirely changing the game. Jennifer Lin | Profile on TED.com Jennifer Lin was only 14 when she performed at TED, drawing tears with her extraordinary improvisation. Onyx Ashanti | Profile on TED.com (http://www.ted.com/speakers/onyx_ashanti.html) Onyx Ashanti is the inventor of "beatjazz"—a new way to music. Raul Midon | Profile on TED.com (http://www.ted.com/speakers/raul_midon.html) Guitarist and singer Raul Midon blends flamenco, jazz and R&B to create a category-defying sound. His life story is as inspiring as his musical vision. About TED | History (http://www.ted.com/pages/16) History of TED itself. Your brain on improv | TED Blog (http://blog.ted.com/2008/03/05/your_brain_on_i/) Two Johns Hopkins researchers have isolated the part of the brain that is most active during improv—the part that Jennifer Lin accesses during her TEDTalk performance. Jennifer Lin on Oprah | TED Blog (http://blog.ted.com/2006/05/09/jennifer_lin_on/) An appearance by the remarkable pianist Jennifer Lin. Hip-hop, creativity and the brain: Q&A with Dr. Charles Limb | TED Blog (http://blog.ted.com/2011/01/18/hip-hop-creativity-and-the-brain-qa-with-dr-charles-limb/) In his TEDTalk (watch now), Charles Limb reviews his groundbreaking work studying creativity and the brain—by putting musicians inside an fMRI and watching as they improvise.

Design

Books and Papers	"A Whole New Mind" by Dan Pink. See also references.
	"The Design of Everyday Things" by Don Norman. See also references.
	"Design is how it Works" by Jay Greene. See also references.
	Cameron, K. (2003). Organizational transformation through architecture and design: a project with Frank Gehry. *Journal of Management Inquiry 12*(1), 88–92.
	Hatchuel, A. (2001). Towards design theory and expandable rationality: the unfinished program of Herbert Simon. *Journal of Management & Governance 5*(3–4), 260–273.
	Norman, D. (2002). *The design of everyday things.* New York, NY: Basic Books.
	Patterson, F. (2004). *Photography and the art of seeing: a visual perception workshop for film and digital photography.* Toronto: Key Porter Books.
	Sloane, J. (2003). Designing. *FSB: Fortune Small Business 13*(9), 92–95.
	Winter, M. (2004). Time and a chair: Teaching design theory. *Human Ecology 32*(1), 6–9 (Social Science Module).
Links	Fast Company: http://www.fastcompany.com/magazine/95/
	Breen, B. (April 1st, 2005). The Business of Design. *Fast Company*
Multi-media	"What is Design?" http://www.youtube.com/watch?v=n7ULeWyBN8w
	Paul Bennett finds design in the details | Video on TED.com (http://www.ted.com/talks/lang/eng/paul_bennett_finds_design_in_the_details.html) Showing a series of inspiring, unusual and playful products, British branding and design guru Paul Bennett explains that design doesn't have to be about grand gestures, but can solve small problems.
	Ross Lovegrove shares organic designs | Video on TED.com (http://www.ted.com/talks/lang/eng/ross_lovegrove_shares_organic_designs.html) Designer Ross Lovegrove expounds his philosophy of "fat-free" design and offers insight into several of his creations.

Paola Antonelli treats design as art | Video on TED.com
(http://www.ted.com/talks/lang/eng/paola_antonelli_treats
_design_as_art.html)
Paola Antonelli, design curator at New York's Museum of Modern
Art, wants to spread her appreciation of design.

Don Norman on 3 ways good design makes you happy | Video on
TED.com
(http://www.ted.com/talks/lang/eng/don_norman_on_design
_and_emotion.html)
In this talk from 2003, design critic Don Norman turns his incisive
eye toward beauty, fun, pleasure and emotion.

John Maeda on his journey in design | Video on TED.com
(http://www.ted.com/talks/lang/eng/john_maeda_on_design
.html)
Designer John Maeda talks about his path from a Seattle tofu
factory to the Rhode Island School of Design.

Tim Brown urges designers to think big | Video on TED.com
(http://www.ted.com/talks/lang/eng/tim_brown_urges
_designers_to_think_big.html)
Tim Brown says the design profession is preoccupied with creating
nifty, fashionable objects.

Stefan Sagmeister shares happy design | Video on TED.com
(http://www.ted.com/talks/lang/eng/stefan_sagmeister_shares
_happy_design.html)
Graphic designer Stefan Sagmeister takes the audience on a
whimsical journey through moments of his life.

David Carson on design + discovery | Video on TED.com
(http://www.ted.com/talks/lang/eng/david_carson_on_design
.html)
Great design is a never-ending journey of discovery -- for which it
helps to pack a healthy sense of humor.

R.A. Mashelkar: Breakthrough designs for ultra-low-cost products
| Video on TED.com
(http://www.ted.com/talks/lang/eng/r_a_mashelkar_break
through_designs_for_ultra_low_cost_products.html)
Engineer RA Mashelkar shares three stories of ultra-low-cost
design from India that use bottom-up rethinking, and some clever
engineering, to bring expensive products to the masses.

Experimentation and Science

Books and Papers	Gleick, J. (1988). *Chaos: making a new science.* Penguin Zukav, G. (2009). *The Dancing Wu Li Masters.* Harper-Collins. Orzel, C. (2009). *How to Teach Physics to Your Dog.* Scribner. "Always be Testing" by Eisenberg et al. 2008
Links	**Big Science** European Organization for Nuclear Research-CERN (http://home.web.cern.ch/about) Lawrence Liverpool National Lab- www.llnl.gov/ **Systems Concepts** http://www.thinking.net/Systems_Thinking/systems_thinking.html
Multi-media	PBS Series: NOVA (http://www.pbs.org/wgbh/nova/) Greene, B. (Host) (October 28th, 2003). Part 1: Einstein's Dream. [Television series episode]. In NOVA (Producer), *The Elegant Universe.* Boston: WGBH/PBS. Holt, S. (Producer & Director) (2003). *Extreme engineering. Boston's big dig* [DVD]. United States: Powderhouse Productions for Discovery Channel. Q&A with Beau Lotto: On seeing yourself see | TED Blog (http://blog.ted.com/2009/10/08/beau_q_and_a/) Neuroscientist and artist Beau Lotto joined the TED Blog for a short Q&A after his 2009 talk from TEDGlobal. He covered some of the fascinating, perception-bending projects. World Science Festival 2009 report: Battlestar Galactica: Cyborgs on the Horizon | TED Blog (http://blog.ted.com/2009/06/15/world_science_f_1/) A young and enthusiastic crowd packed the 92nd Street Y on Friday night to enjoy yet another reunion of science and art at the World Science Festival. Sam Harris: Science can answer moral questions | TED Talk (http://www.ted.com/talks/sam_harris_science_can_show_what_s_right.html)

Aesthetics

Books and Papers	Ewenstein, B., & Whyte, J. (2007). Beyond words: Aesthetic knowledge and knowing in organizations. *Organization Studies 28(5)*, 689–708. Gibb, S. (2004). Imagination, creativity, and HRD: An aesthetic perspective. *Human Resource Development Review 3*(1), 53–74. Gorawara-Bhat, R. (2001). Organization and aesthetics [review of the book *Organization and Aesthetics*]. *Contemporary Sociology 30*(1), 34–35. Merritt, S. (2010). What does beauty have to do with business? *The Journal of Business Strategy 31*(4), 70–76. Strati, A. (1999). *Organization and aesthetics* (1st ed.). Thousand Oaks: Sage Publications. Vince, R. (2001). Organisation and aesthetics [review of the book *Organization and Aesthetics*]. *Management Learning 32*(1), 135–137.
Links	http://www.iep.utm.edu/aestheti/
Multi-media	Frank Gehry http://www.pbs.org/wnet/americanmasters/episodes/frank-gehry/sketches-of-frank-gehry/602/ Vik Muniz | Profile on TED.com (http://www.ted.com/speakers/vik_muniz.html) Brazilian-born, Brooklyn-based fine artist Vik Muniz has exhibited his work all over the world. Using unexpected materials to create portraits, landscapes and still lifes. Adam Sadowsky | Profile on TED.com (http://www.ted.com/speakers/adam_sadowsky.html) As the president of Syyn Labs, Adam Sadowsky merges art and technology to create interactive projects big and small. Raghava KK | Profile on TED.com (http://www.ted.com/speakers/kk_raghava.html) Raghava KK's paintings and drawings use cartoonish shapes and colors to examine the body, society, our world.

TED Conferences | Past TEDs | TED2004
(http://www.ted.com/pages/55)
TED is not just about psychology, or evolution or economics
or the environment or entertainment or aesthetics or mysticism.
They're about the whole interwoven human experience.

Robert Lang | Profile on TED.com
(http://www.ted.com/speakers/robert_lang.html)
Robert Lang merges mathematics with aesthetics to fold elegant
modern origami. His scientific approach helps him make folds
once thought impossible.

Nancy Etcoff | Profile on TED.com
(http://www.ted.com/speakers/nancy_etcoff.html)
Nancy Etcoff is part of a new vanguard of cognitive researchers
asking: What makes us happy? Why do we like beautiful things?
And how on earth did we evolve that way?

Reed Kroloff | Profile on TED.com
(http://www.ted.com/speakers/reed_kroloff.html)
With an outspoken approach to the problems of rebuilding cites
and a fearless eye for design, Reed Kroloff is helping to change the
urban landscape of cities from New York to New Orleans.

TED and Reddit asked Sir Ken Robinson anything—and he
answered | TED Blog
(http://blog.ted.com/2009/08/12/ted_and_reddit_1/)
For the first in a new series of community-driven Q&As, TED
and Reddit joined forces to ask creativity expert Sir Ken Robinson
any question.

Fellows Friday with Andy Amadi Okoroafor | TED Blog
(http://blog.ted.com/2010/12/24/fellows-friday-with-andy-
amadi-okoroafor/)
Andy Amadi Okoroafor, founder of creative studio Clam, loves
to use imagery in different ways, from fashion to film. Here, he
reveals how shortwave radio influences his work.

Q&A with Bjarke Ingels: On architectural alchemy | TED Blog
(http://blog.ted.com/2009/10/30/qa_with_bjarke/)
The TED Blog caught up with Bjarke Ingels several weeks after he
gave his TEDTalk at TEDGlobal 2009.

Human Strengths, Creativity and Intelligence

| Books and Papers | **Creativity**
Free Play by Stephen Nachmanovich
Creativity in Business by Ray and Meyers
Drawing on the right side of the brain by Betty Edwards
Linchpin: Are You Indispensable? by Seth Godin

Multiple Intelligences (MI)
Anonymous. (2005). Understanding the Theory of Multiple Intelligences. *Scholastic Early Childhood Today 20*(3), 13–14.

Acar, E., Wall, J., McNamee, F., Carney, M., & Öney-Yazici, E. (2008). Innovative safety management training through e-learning. *Architectural Engineering and Design Management 4*(3/4), 239–250.

Chan, D. W. (2007). Components of leadership giftedness and multiple intelligences among Chinese gifted students in Hong Kong. *High Ability Studies 18*(2), 155–172.

Green, A., Hill, A., Friday, E., & Friday, S. (2005). The use of multiple intelligences to enhance team productivity. *Management Decision 43*(3), 349–359.

Martin, J. (2005). *Profiting from multiple intelligences in the workplace*. Norwalk, CT: Crown House Publishing Limited.

Shearer, C., & Luzzo, D. (2009). Exploring the Application of Multiple Intelligences Theory to Career Counseling. *The Career Development Quarterly 58*(1), 3–13.

Weller, D. (1999). Application of the multiple intelligences theory in quality organizations. *Team Performance Management 5*(4), 136. |
| Links | **Multiple Intelligence Theory and Measurement**
http://www.thirteen.org/edonline/concept2class/mi/
http://www.bgfl.org/custom/resources_ftp/client_ftp/ks3/ict/multiple_int/questions/choose_lang.cfm
Howard Gardner
http://www.infed.org/thinkers/gardner.htm
General IQ
http://www.aceintelligence.com/index.php
Myers-Briggs
http://www.myersbriggs.org/
http://www.personalitypathways.com/type_inventory.html |

Multi-media	*Brain Power* (1990 VHS). (Available from MTI Business & Industry Group, 5130 Industrial Street, Maple Plain, MN 55359).
	Gardner, H. (Producer) (1998). *Creativity & Leadership: Making the Mind Extraordinary* (VHS). (Available from Into the Classroom Media, 10573 W. Pico Blvd., Los Angeles, CA 90064)
	Anderson, C. (Founder). (February 27th, 2004). Mihaly Csikszentmihalyi on flow. [Web video series episode]. In C. Anderson (Curator), *TED*. Monterey, CA: TED2004. Retrieved from: http://www.ted.com/index.php/talks/lang/eng /mihaly_csikszentmihalyi_on_flow.html
	Joshua Klein on the intelligence of crows | Video on TED.com (http://www.ted.com/talks/lang/eng/joshua_klein_on_the _intelligence_of_crows.html) Hacker and writer Joshua Klein is fascinated by crows. After a long amateur study of corvid behavior, he's come up with elegant insights.
	Jeff Hawkins | Profile on TED.com (http://www.ted.com/speakers/jeff_hawkins.html) Jeff Hawkins pioneered the development of PDAs such as the Palm and Treo. Now he's trying to understand how the human brain really works.
	Matt Ridley | Profile on TED.com (http://www.ted.com/speakers/matt_ridley.html) Matt Ridley argues that, through history, the engine of human progress and prosperity has been, and is, "ideas having sex with each other."
	Dan Dennett | Profile on TED.com (http://www.ted.com/speakers/dan_dennett.html) Philosopher and scientist Dan Dennett argues that human consciousness and free will are the result of physical processes and are not what we traditionally think they are.
	Stuart Brown | Profile on TED.com (http://www.ted.com/speakers/stuart_brown.html) Stuart Brown's research shows play is not just joyful and energizing— it's deeply involved with human development and intelligence.

Susan Savage-Rumbaugh | Profile on TED.com
(http://www.ted.com/speakers/susan_savage_rumbaugh.html)
Susan Savage-Rumbaugh has made startling breakthroughs in her lifelong work with chimpanzees and bonobos, showing the animals to be adept in picking up language and other "intelligent" behaviors.

Deb Roy | Profile on TED.com
(http://www.ted.com/speakers/deb_roy.html)
Deb Roy studies how children learn language, and designs machines that learn to communicate in human-like ways. On sabbatical from MIT Media Lab, he's working with the AI company Bluefin Labs.

Marvin Minsky | Profile on TED.com
(http://www.ted.com/speakers/marvin_minsky.html)
Marvin Minsky is one of the great pioneers of artificial intelligence—and using computing metaphors to understand the human mind.

Krista Tippett | Profile on TED.com
(http://www.ted.com/speakers/krista_tippett.html)
Krista Tippett hosts the national public radio program "On Being" (formerly "Speaking of Faith"), which takes up the great animating questions of human life: What does it mean to be human?

Allison Hunt | Profile on TED.com
(http://www.ted.com/speakers/allison_hunt.html)
Allison Hunt has worked in advertising and marketing for 20 years, developing human insight and persuasion into an art for her clients. She found these skills came in very handy.

Learning and Constructivism

Books and Papers	All, A., & Brandon, A. (2010). Constructivism theory analysis and application to curricula. *Nursing Education Perspectives 31*(2), 89–92.
	Altman, B. (2009). Determining US worker's training: history and constructivist paradigm. *Journal of European Industrial Training 33*(6), 480–491.
	Chen, I., & Liu, C. (2010). Evolution of Constructivism. *Contemporary Issues in Education Research 3*(4), 63–66.

	Cottone, R. (2001). A social constructivism model of ethical decision making in counseling. *Journal of Counseling and Development 79*(1), 39–45.
	Kalina, C., & Powell, K. (2009). Cognitive and social constructivism: developing tools for an effective classroom. *Education 130*(2), 241–249.
	Prakash, E. (2010). Explicit constructivism: a missing link in ineffective lectures? *Advances in Physiology Education 34*(1), 93–96.
	Sakulbumrungsil, R., Sthapornnanon, N., Theeraroungchaisiri, A., & Watcharadamrongkun, S. (2009). Social constructivist learning environment in an online professional practice course. *American Journal of Pharmaceutical Education 73*(1), 1–8.
Multi-media	Sir Ken Robinson: Bring on the learning revolution! | Video on TED.com (http://www.ted.com/talks/lang/eng/sir_ken_robinson_bring_on_the_revolution.html) Sir Ken Robinson makes the case for a radical shift from standardized schools to personalized learning—creating conditions where kids' natural talents can flourish.
	David Merrill demos Siftables | Video on TED.com (http://www.ted.com/talks/lang/eng/david_merrill_demos_siftables_the_smart_blocks.html) Is this the next thing in hands-on learning?
	Chris Anderson: How web video powers global innovation | Video on TED.com (http://www.ted.com/talks/lang/eng/chris_anderson_how_web_video_powers_global_innovation.html) Video is driving a worldwide phenomenon he calls Crowd Accelerated Innovation -- a self-fueling cycle of learning that could be as significant as the invention of print.
	Ali Carr-Chellman: Gaming to re-engage boys in learning | Video on TED.com (http://www.ted.com/talks/lang/eng/ali_carr_chellman_gaming_to_re_engage_boys_in_learning.html) At TEDxPSU, Ali Carr-Chellman pinpoints three reasons boys are tuning out of school in droves, and lays out her bold plan to re-engage them: bringing their culture into the classroom.

Aditi Shankardass: A second opinion on learning disorders | Video on TED.com
(http://www.ted.com/talks/lang/eng/aditi_shankardass_a_second_opinion_on_learning_disorders.html)
Developmental disorders in children are typically diagnosed by observing behavior, but Aditi Shankardass knew that we should be looking directly at their brains.

Ben Dunlap talks about a passionate life | Video on TED.com
(http://www.ted.com/talks/lang/eng/ben_dunlap_talks_about_a_passionate_life.html)
Sandor Teszler is a Hungarian Holocaust survivor who taught Dunlop about passionate living and lifelong learning.

Srikumar Rao: Plug into your hard-wired happiness | Video on TED.com
(http://www.ted.com/talks/lang/eng/srikumar_rao_plug_into_your_hard_wired_happiness.html)
Srikumar Rao says we spend most of our lives learning to be unhappy, even as we strive for happiness.

Arvind Gupta: Turning trash into toys for learning | Video on TED.com
(http://www.ted.com/talks/lang/eng/arvind_gupta_turning_trash_into_toys_for_learning.html)
About how to turn trash into seriously entertaining, well-designed toys that kids can build themselves—while learning basic principles of science and design.

Caleb Chung plays with Pleo | Video on TED.com
(http://www.ted.com/talks/lang/eng/caleb_chung_plays_with_pleo.html)
Pleo the robot dinosaur acts like a living pet—exploring, cuddling, playing, reacting and learning. Inventor Caleb Chung talks about Pleo and his wild toy career.

World Views and Behavioral Change

	World Views
Books and Papers	**Mental Models** A good book on world views, mental models and wisdom is: "Seeking Wisdom: From Darwin to Munger" by Peter Bevelin **Time Management** "The 4-Hour Workweek" by Tim Ferriss. A must read for anyone living in the 21st century **Creativity** Ray, M., & Myers, R. (2000). *Creativity in business.* New York, NY: Broadway Books. **Chaos Theory:** Gleick, J. (1988). *Chaos: making a new science.* New York, NY: Penguin.
Multimedia	Ken Robinson says schools kill creativity | Video on TED.com (http://www.ted.com/talks/lang/eng/ken_robinson_says_schools _kill_creativity.html) A profoundly moving case for creating an education system that nurtures (rather than undermines) creativity. Adora Svitak: What adults can learn from kids | Video on TED .com (http://www.ted.com/talks/lang/eng/adora_svitak.html) Child prodigy Adora Svitak says the world needs "childish" thinking: bold ideas, wild creativityand especially optimism. Shekhar Kapur: We are the stories we tell ourselves | Video on TED.com (http://www.ted.com/talks/lang/eng/shekhar_kapur_we_are_the _stories_we_tell_ourselves.html) Hollywood/Bollywood director Shekhar Kapur ("Elizabeth," "Mr. India") pinpoints his source of creativity: sheer, utter panic. He shares a powerful way to unleash your inner storyteller. Jennifer Lin improvs piano magic | Video on TED.com (http://www.ted.com/talks/lang/eng/jennifer_lin_improvs_piano _magic.html) Pianist and composer Jennifer Lin gives a magical performance, talks about the process ofcreativity and improvises a moving solo piece based on a random sequence of notes.

Malcolm McLaren: Authentic creativity vs. karaoke culture | Video on TED.com
(http://www.ted.com/talks/lang/eng/malcolm_mclaren_authentic_creativity_vs_karaoke_culture.html)
How does one find authentic creativity? In his last talk before passing away, Malcolm McLaren tells remarkable stories from his own life.

Isaac Mizrahi on fashion and creativity | Video on TED.com
(http://www.ted.com/talks/lang/eng/isaac_mizrahi_on_fashion_and_creativity.html)
Fashion designer Isaac Mizrahi spins through a dizzying array of inspirations -- from '50s pinups to a fleeting glimpse of a woman on the street who makes him shout "Stop the cab!"

Elizabeth Gilbert on nurturing creativity | Video on TED.com
(http://www.ted.com/talks/lang/eng/elizabeth_gilbert_on_genius.html)
Elizabeth Gilbert muses on the impossible things we expect from artists and geniuses -- and shares the radical idea that, instead of the rare person "being" a genius, all of us "have" a genius.

Larry Lessig on laws that choke creativity | Video on TED.com
(http://www.ted.com/talks/lang/eng/larry_lessig_says_the_law_is_strangling_creativity.html)
Larry Lessig, the Net's most celebrated lawyer, cites John Philip Sousa, celestial copyrights and the "ASCAP cartel" in his argument for reviving our creative culture.

Henry Markram builds a brain in a supercomputer | Video on TED.com
(http://www.ted.com/talks/lang/eng/henry_markram_supercomputing_the_brain_s_secrets.html)
Henry Markram says the mysteries of the mind can be solved—soon. Mental illness, memory, perception: they're made of neurons and electric signals, and he plans to find them with a supercomputer.

10 ways the world could end: Stephen Petranek on TED.com | TED Blog
(http://blog.ted.com/2007/09/25/stephen_petrane/)
Stephen Petranek reveals the question that occupies scientists at the end of the day (and the beginning of happy hour): How might the world end? He lays out the challenges that face us.

	Struggling with quantum logic: Q&A with Aaron O'Connell | TED Blog (http://blog.ted.com/2011/06/02/struggling-with-quantum-logic-qa-with-aaron-oconnell/) On stage at TED2011, Aaron O'Connell talked about building the largest object ever put into a quantum mechanical state, a vibrating piece of metal (called a mechanical resonator).

Gaming and Innovation

	Gaming
Books and Papers	Cohendet, P., Grandadam, D., & Simon, L. (2010). The Anatomy of the Creative City. *Industry and Innovation 17*(1), 91–111.
	Cohendet, P., & Simon, L. (2007). Playing across the playground: paradoxes of knowledge creation in the videogame firm. *Journal of Organizational Behavior 28*(5), 587–605.
	Larach, U., & Cabra, J. (2010). Creative problem solving in Second Life: an action research study. *Creativity and Innovation Management 19*(2), 167–179.
	Lopez-Paceco, A. (2010). Creativity is key to profitability. *Financial Post.* Retrieved from http://www.financialpost.com/executive/Creativity+profitability/3656072/story.html
	Salmon, G. (2009). The future for (second) life and learning. *British Journal of Educational Technology 40*(3), 526–538.
	Tschang, F. (2007). Balancing the tensions between rationalization and creativity in the video games industry. *Organization Science 18*(6), 989–1005, 1023.
Multimedia	Jesse Schell: When games invade real life | Video on TED.com (http://www.ted.com/talks/lang/eng/jesse_schell_when_games_invade_real_life.html) Games are invading the real world -- and the runaway popularity of Farmville and Guitar Hero is just the beginning.
	Tom Chatfield: 7 ways games reward the brain | Video on TED.com (http://www.ted.com/talks/lang/eng/tom_chatfield_7_ways_games_reward_the_brain.html) Tom Chatfield shows that games are perfectly tuned to dole out rewards that engage the brain and keep us questing for more.

Tod Machover and Dan Ellsey play new music | Video on TED.com
(http://www.ted.com/talks/lang/eng/tod_machover_and_dan
_ellsey_play_new_music.html)

Brenda Laurel on games for girls | Video on TED.com
(http://www.ted.com/talks/lang/eng/brenda_laurel_on_making
_games_for_girls.html)
A TED archive gem. At TED in 1998, Brenda Laurel asks: Why
are all the top-selling video games aimed at little boys? She spent
two years researching the world of girls.

David Perry: Are games better than life? | Video on TED.com
(http://www.ted.com/talks/lang/eng/david_perry_on_videogames
.html)
Game designer David Perry says tomorrow's videogames will be
more than mere fun to the next generation of gamers. They'll be
lush, complex, emotional.

Stuart Brown says play is more than fun | Video on TED.com
(http://www.ted.com/talks/lang/eng/stuart_brown_says_play_is
_more_than_fun_it_s_vital.html)
A pioneer in research on play, Dr. Stuart Brown says humor, games,
roughhousing, flirtation and fantasy are more than just fun.

Jane McGonigal: Gaming can make a better world | Video on
TED.com
(http://www.ted.com/talks/lang/eng/jane_mcgonigal_gaming
_can_make_a_better_world.html)
Games like World of Warcraft give players the means to save
worlds, and incentive to learn the habits of heros.

Beau Lotto: Optical illusions show how we see | Video on TED
.com
(http://www.ted.com/talks/lang/eng/beau_lotto_optical_illusions
_show_how_we_see.html)
Beau Lotto's color games puzzle your vision, but they also spotlight
what you can't normally see: how your brain works.

John Hunter on the World Peace Game | Video on TED.com
(http://www.ted.com/talks/lang/eng/john_hunter_on_the
_world_peace_game.html)
John Hunter puts all the problems of the world on a 4'x5' plywood
board -- and lets his 4th-graders solve them. At TED2011, he
explains how his World Peace Game engages school kids.

Notes

Chapter 1

1. Porter (1980), pp. 34–46.
2. I highly recommend an excellent book on this means of learning. Schon (1983).
3. Ernst (1991), p. 102.
4. Ernst (1991), p. 102.
5. Argyris and Schon (1978).

Chapter 2

1. Stanford University (2005).
2. Aerts et al. (2007).
3. Table adapted from Aerts et al. (2007).
4. The authors pose two additional somewhat esoteric questions: (1) How are we to construct our image of this world in such a way that we can come up with answers to the preceding, and (2) What are some of the partial answers that we can propose to these questions?
5. Simon (1969). The word artificial is used in contrast to the "natural world."
6. Pink (2005).
7. See, for example, Ray and Meyers (1986).
8. The original: "You are not really trying until you have failed or gone out of business several times."
9. See also, Ray and Myers (1986).
10. See also, Ray and Myers (1986).
11. Suzuki (1970).
12. Herrigel (1953).
13. Hint: Begin the sentence with "Yes, but ...." Note: there is one other even better way to begin the sentence. What is it?

Chapter 3

1. Hernstein and Murray (1994).
2. Neisser et al. (1996).
3. Neisser et al. (1996), p. 83.

4. Deary, Strand, Smith, and Fernandes (2007), p. 18.
5. Deary, Strand, Smith, and Fernandes (2007).
6. Frey and Detteman (2004).
7. As derived from the Armed Services Vocational Aptitude Battery.
8. As measured by the Ravens Advanced Progressive Matrices instrument.
9. Gardner (1994); Gardner (1996); Gardner (1998a); Gardner (1998b).
10. Gardner notes that although some of the people above such as Mozart were prodigies as children, many did not attain greatness until much later in life.
11. All photos included in Table 3.3 are in the public domain in the United States and elsewhere.
12. Considered a half-intelligence. Descartes is shown here as an example provided by the author, not Gardner.
13. Chase and Simon (1973).
14. Gardner (1994); Gardner (1996); Gardner (1998a); Gardner (1998b).
15. Gladwell (2008).
16. See also Gardner (1998a); Gardner (1998b).
17. Links to these sites change frequently. Here are a few MI assessment links to get you started: http://www.literacyworks.org/mi/assessment/findyour strengths.html; http://www.bgfl.org/custom/resources_ftp/client_ftp/ks3/ ict/multiple_int/questions/questions.cfm
18. The following improvement was made after only 1 hour of training in technique!
19. Image courtesy of the author. Eric W. Stein. All rights reserved. Reference: ericwstein.com.
20. The number of 2D MI combinations (e.g., 28) is calculated as $8!/((6!)*(2!))$. The number of composites of the three top MI areas (out of the eight) is $8!/ ((5!)*(3!)) = 56$ combinations.

Chapter 4

1. Lunsford (2009).
2. See, for example, http://www.thefreedictionary.com/improvise
3. Berliner (1994), p. 241.
4. Barrett (1998), p. 606.
5. Berliner (1994) p. 492; as noted by Weick (1998).
6. C. Mingus appearing in Kernfeld (1995), p. 119 as cited by Weick (1998).
7. Weick (1998).
8. Konitz cited in Berliner (1994), p. 193 as cited by Weick (1998).
9. Drucker (1985).
10. Luecke and Katz (2003), p. 2.
11. All photos shown are public domain unless otherwise noted.

12. Author: Tom Palumbo from New York City, USA. This image licensed under the Creative Commons Attribution-Share Alike Generic license, which allows it to be freely shared or remixed. Reference: http://en.wikipedia.org/wiki/File:Miles_Davis_by_Palumbo.jpg

13. Images of the founders unavailable. A public domain image of a network connection is provided instead.

14. Author: guillaumepaumier.com, CC-BY. This file is licensed under the Creative Commons Attribution 3.0 Unported license. Reference: http://en.wikipedia.org/wiki/File:Mark_Zuckerberg_at_the_37th_G8_Summit_in_Deauville_018_v1.jpg

15. YCharts (2013); Cisco (2013).

16. Interesting work is being done looking at the creative characteristics of people in real-time simulated environments and the degree to which design thinking and improvisation are facilitated. See, for example, Stein, Reychav, and Ben-Eliezer (2014).

17. Simon (1960).

18. A framework that was subsequently used to categorize Decision Support Systems. See, for example, Gorry and Morton (1971).

19. As defined by Jones (1991).

20. Jones (1991), p. 374.

21. See Stein (2011). Reproduced with kind permission from Springer Science+Business Media B.V.

22. Stein and Ahmad (2009).

23. Weick (1998) quoting Berliner (1994), p. 400.

24. Emery and Trist (1965).

25. See Stein (2011). Reproduced with kind permission from Springer Science+Business Media B.V.

Chapter 5

1. *Source:* The American Heritage Dictionary of the English Language. http://www.ahdictionary.com/word/search.html?q=design&submit.x=-664&submit.y=-210

2. Creativity is a broad subject that can mean many things. Design is a specific, measurable instance of creativity. Throughout this book, I highlight specific behaviors associated with creativity.

3. Hooker (2004).

4. Simon (1960).

5. Jonassen (2000), p. 14.

6. Jonassen (2000), p. 14.

7. Anyone who has suffered through the screen-writer strikes over the years realized how un-funny most comedians are without their writers. Unless the comedian is gifted in improvisational comedy, without a script, he or she will fail miserably in front of audiences.
8. From Jonassen (2000), p. 14.
9. Gardner (1998a); Gardner (1998b).
10. All images are public domain unless otherwise noted.
11. Image Author: Uldis Bojārs. This file is licensed under the Creative Commons Attribution-Share Alike 2.0 Generic license. Reference: http://en.wikipedia.org/wiki/File:Tim_Berners-Lee.jpg
12. Author: Marcus Dawes. http://www.marcusdawes.com. This file is licensed under the Creative Commons Attribution-Share Alike 3.0 Unported license. Reference: http://en.wikipedia.org/wiki/File:Jonathan_Ive_(OTRS).jpg
13. http://www.w3.org/People/Berners-Lee/
14. Internet World Stats.
15. Businessweek (2006).
16. Fortune (2010).
17. Statistic Brain (2012).
18. Gardner (1998a); Gardner (1998b). See also Figure 3.1 in Chapter 3.
19. Apple licensed this technology from Xerox, which was unable to commercialize it for mass market.
20. Hatchuel (2001), p. 270.
21. Hatchuel (2001).
22. Brown (2007).
23. Tim Brown as quoted by Hansen (2010).
24. Greene (2010), p. 119.
25. Greene (2010), p. 121.
26. Greene (2010), p. 98.
27. *Source:* Csikszentmihalyi (1996).
28. Author: Eric W. Stein. All rights reserved. Permission granted for this work. Reference: ericwstein.com
29. Csikszentmihalyi (2004).
30. Based on work by Csikszentmihalyi (1996); Csikszentmihalyi (2004).
31. National Endowment for the Arts (n.d.).
32. Bloomberg/Businessweek (2009).
33. *Source:* http://www.mpd.cmu.edu/curriculum.htm

Chapter 6

1. Morris (1992).
2. Gottlieb (1997).

3. For an excellent discussion of the mental models that undergird the pursuit of scientific knowledge, see Popper (2002) and Kuhn (1996).

4. Chaos theory is a historical oddity. Although discovered in the 1880s, it was not until the 1960s with the invention of the computer that significant progress was made on the theory.

5. All images in the public domain unless otherwise noted.

6. The macroscopic scale is the length scale on which objects or processes are of a size which is measurable and observable by the naked eye. It is our everyday world of experience.

7. Webster's New World (2010).

8. BrainyQuote (2011).

9. Gleick (1987).

10. The speed of light is 186,000 miles per second.

11. *Source:* http://en.wikipedia.org/wiki/File:Doubleslit.svg. Author: Ebohr1. svg. This file is licensed under the Creative Commons Attribution-Share Alike 3.0 Unported license.

12. See, for example, Kumar (2011).

13. Interestingly, there is a link between scientific experimentation and aesthetics as will be noted later in the book.

14. See, for example, Brown (2008).

15. Tulley (2009).

16. Schon (1983).

Chapter 7

1. Harper (2010).

2. Stanford University (2005).

3. Gibb (2004); Beardsley (1966).

4. Author: roseoftimothywood. Reference: http://commons.wikimedia.org/wiki/File:Mirror_baby.jpg. This file is licensed under the Creative Commons Attribution 2.0 Generic license.

5. Gorawara-Bhat (2001).

6. Gibb (2004), p. 67.

7. All images in the public domain unless otherwise noted.
   Image B author: Veronica Therese. This file is licensed under the Creative Commons Attribution-Share Alike 3.0 Unported license. Reference: http://en.wikipedia.org/wiki/File:OpenPlanRedBalloon1.jpg

   Image D author: This file is licensed under the Creative Commons Attribution-Share Alike 2.0 Generic license. Reference: http://en.wikipedia.org/wiki/File:CubeSpace.jpg

   Image F author: Ashstar01. Google Mt View campus garden. This file is licensed under the Creative Commons Attribution-Share Alike 3.0

Unported license. Reference: http://en.wikipedia.org/wiki/File:Google_Mountain_View_campus_garden.jpg

8. All images public domain unless otherwise noted. Image of Apple iPod authored by Stahlkocher. Reference: http://en.wikipedia.org/wiki/File:Ipod_5th_Generation_white.jpg. This file is licensed under the Creative Commons Attribution-Share Alike 3.0 Unported license.

9. Norman (2002), p. 153.

10. Gibb (2004).

11. Gibb (2004), p. 4.

12. Strati (1999); Gorawara-Bhat (2001).

Chapter 8

1. Argyris and Schon (1978).

2. I have attended several great workshops over the years: the Aebersold Jazz workshop in Louisville, Kentucky, the New York Jazz Academy in New York City, and the Stanford Jazz workshop in Palo Alto, California, for example. One workshop I attended (Jazz Camp West) was held in a redwood forest near Santa Cruz, California.

3. This is an illustration. Always consult your doctor before making lifestyle changes.

4. Ferriss (2007).

5. Don't fall into the trap of "Us versus Them" thinking.

6. Obviously, performing in a professional context carries a higher degree of risk and will require more preparation.

7. Festinger (1957).

8. Title: "Tendril of an unidentified climber plant near Orosí, Costa Rica." Author: Dirk van der Made. This file is licensed under the Creative Commons Attribution-Share Alike 3.0 Unported license. Reference: http://en.wikipedia.org/wiki/File:DirkvdM_natural_spiral.jpg

9. Jobs (2005).

10. This quote can be attributed to Audre Lorde (1934–1992), who was a writer, poet, and activist. My friend is Dr. Jaime Alonzo Gomez, a fellow graduate of the Wharton School of the University of Pennsylvania and former Dean of the School of Business at the Monterrey Institute of Technology (Mexico) and currently professor at the University of San Diego.

Appendix

1. Links on the web are subject to change and over which, the author has no control.

References

Aerts et al. (2007). *World Views* (Internet Edition). Brussels: VUB Press.

Argyris, C., & Schon, D. A. (1978). *Organizational learning: A Theory of action perspective*. Reading, MA: Addison-Wesley.

Barrett, F. (1998). Creativity and improvisation in jazz and organizations: Implications for organizational learning. *Organization Science 9*(5), 606–622.

Beardsley, M. C. (1966). *Aesthetics from classical Greece to the present*. London: University of Alabama Press.

Berliner, P. (1994). *Thinking in jazz: The infinite art of improvisation*. Chicago, IL: University of Chicago.

Bloomberg/Businessweek. (2009, September 30). *Special report: Design thinking*. Retrieved March 8, 2011, from Bloomberg/Businessweek: http://www.businessweek.com/innovate/di_special/20090930design_thinking.htm

BrainyQuote. (2011). *Murray Gell-Mann Quotes*. Retrieved March 2011, from BrainyQuote: http://www.brainyquote.com/quotes/authors/m/murray_gellmann.html

Brown, T. (2007, December 19). *Strategy by design*. Retrieved February 1, 2011, from FastCompany.com: www.fastcompany.com/magazine/95/design-strategy.html

Brown, J. S. (2008). *John Seely Brown: Tinkering as a mode of knowledge production*. Retrieved 2013, from Youtube.com: http://youtu.be/9u-MczVpkUA

Burrows, P. (2006, September 25). *Who Is Jonathan Ive?* Retrieved March 2, 2011, from www.businessweek.com: http://www.businessweek.com/magazine/content/06_39/b4002414.htm

Chase, W., & Simon, H. (1973). Perception in Chess. *Cognitive Psychology 4*, 55–81.

Cisco. (2013). *Cisco reports fourth quarter and fiscal year 2013 earnings*. Retrieved August 14, 2013, from Newsroom.cisco.com: http://newsroom.cisco.com/press-release-content?articleId=1236468

Csikszentmihalyi, M. (1996). *Creativity*. New York, NY: Harper Collins.

Csikszentmihalyi, M. (2004). *TED Talks: Mihaly Csikszentmihalyi: Creativity, fulfillment and flow*. Retrieved 2011, from YouTube: http://www.youtube.com/watch?v=fXIeFJCqsPs&playnext=1&list=PL5EE8EAA551ED6420

Deary, I., Strand, S., Smith, S., & Fernandes, C. (2007). Intelligence and educational achievement. *Intelligence 35*, 13–21.

Drucker, P. (1985). *Innovation and entrepreneurship*. New York, NY: Harper and Row.

Emery, F., & Trist, E. (1965). The causal texture of organizational environments. *Human Relations, 18,* 21–32.

Ernst, P. (1991). *The philosophy of mathematics education.* London: Routledge-Falmer.

Ferriss, T. (2007). *The 4–hour work week: Escape the 9–5, live anywhere and join the new rich.* New York, NY: Crown.

Festinger, L. (1957). *A theory of cognitive dissonance.* Stanford, Palo Alto, CA: Stanford University Press.

Fortune. (2010). *The smartest people in tech.* Retrieved March 2, 2011, from Fortune: http://money.cnn.com/galleries/2010/technology/1007/gallery.smartest_people_tech.fortune/6.html

Frey, M., & Detterman, D. (2004). Scholastic Assessment or g? The relationship between the Scholastic Assessment Test and general cognitive ability. *Psychological Science 15*(6), 373–378.

Gardner, H. (1994). *Creating minds: An anatomy of creativity as seen through the lives of Freud, Einstein, Picasso, Stravinsky, Eliot, Graham, and Gandhi.* New York, NY: Basic Books.

Gardner, H. (1996). *Leading minds: An anatomy of leadership.* New York, NY: Basic Books.

Gardner, H. (1998a). *Extraordinary minds: Portraits of 4 exceptional individuals and an examination of our own extraordinariness.* New York, NY: Basic Books.

Gardner, H. (Director). (1998b). *Creativity & leadership: Making the mind extraordinary* [Motion Picture]. Los Angeles, CA

Gibb, S. (2004). Imagination, creativity, and HRD: An aesthetic perspective. *Human Resource Development Review 3*(1), 53–75.

Gladwell, M. (2008). *Outliers: The story of success.* New York: Little, Brown and Company.

Gleick, J. (1987). *Chaos: Making of a new science.* New York, NY: Penguin.

Gorawara-Bhat, R. (2001). Organization and Aesthetics (Book Review). *Contemporary Sociology 30*(1), 34–36.

Gorry, A., & Morton, M. S. (1971). A Framework for Management Information Systems. *Sloan Management Review,* 458–470.

Gottlieb, S. (1997, April 8). *What is Science?* Retrieved March 2011, from Harbinger: http://www.theharbinger.org/articles/rel_sci/gottlieb.html

Greene, J. (2010). *Design is how it works.* New York, NY: Penguin.

Hansen, M. T. (2010, January/February). *IDEO CEO Tim Brown: T-Shaped Stars: The Backbone of IDEO's Collaborative Culture.* Retrieved February 1, 2011, from ChiefExecutive.net: http://chiefexecutive.net/ME2/dirmod.asp?sid=&nm=&type=Publishing&mod=Publications::Article&mid=8F3A7027421841978F18BE895F87F791&tier=4&id=F42A23CB49174C5E9426C43CB0A0BC46

Harper, D. (2010). http://www.etymonline.com/index.php?term=aesthetics. Retrieved 12/7/2010, from the Online Etymology Dictionary: www.etymonline.com

Hatchuel, A. (2001). Towards design theory and expandable rationality: The unfinished program of Herbert Simon. *Journal of Management & Governance*, 260–273.

Herrigel, E. (1953). *Zen in the art of archery*. New York, NY: Pantheon Books.

Hernstein, R., & Murray, C. (1994). *The bell curve*. New York, NY: Free Press.

Hooker, J. N. (2004). Is design theory possible? *Journal of Information Technology Theory and Application 6*(2), 73–83.

Jobs, S. (2005, June 14). *Stanford report*. Retrieved 2013, from Stanford News: http://news.stanford.edu/news/2005/june15/jobs-061505.html

Jonassen, D. H. (2000). Toward a design theory of problem solving. *Educational, Technology, Research and Development 48*(4), 63–86.

Jones, T. M. (1991). Ethical decision making by individuals in organizations. *The Academy of Management Review 16*(2), 366–395.

Kuhn, Thomas S. *The structure of scientific revolutions*. 3rd ed. Chicago, IL: University of Chicago Press, 1996.

Kumar, M. (2011). *Quantum: Einstein, Bohr, and the Great Debate about the nature of reality*. New York, NY: Norton.

Luecke, R., & Katz, R. (2003). *Managing creativity and innovation*. Boston, MA: Harvard Business School Press.

Lunsford, L. (2009, January 16). *Praise heaped on veteran airman for pulling off rare feat*. Retrieved November 29, 2010, from Wall Street Journal Online: http://online.wsj.com/article/SB123205611103787217.html

Morris, C. G. (1992). *Academic press dictionary of science and technology*. New York, NY: Harcourt.

National Endowment for the Arts. (n.d.). *Fahrenheit 451: About the author*. Retrieved March 2, 2011, from National Endowment for the Arts: http://www.neabigread.org/books/fahrenheit451/fahrenheit451_04.php

Neisser et al. (1996). Intelligence: Knowns and unknowns. *American Psychologist 51*(2), 77–101.

Norman, D. A. (2002). *The design of everyday things*. New York, NY: Basic Books.

Pink, D. (2005). *A whole new mind*. New York, NY: Riverhead.

Popper, Karl (2002). *The logic of scientific discovery*, New York: Routledge Classics

Porter, M. (1980). *Competitive strategy*. New York, NY: The Free Press.

Ray, M., & Meyers, R. (1986). *Creativity in business*. New York, NY: Broadway Books (Random House).

Schon, D. (1983). *The reflective practitioner: How professionals think in action*. London: Temple Smith.

Simon, H. (1960). *The new science of management decision*. New York, NY: Harper and Row.

Simon, H. (1969). *The sciences of the artificial*. Cambridge, Mass: MIT Press.

Stanford University. (2005). *Kant's aesthetics and teleology*. Retrieved December 7, 2010, from Stanford Encyclopedia of Philosophy: http://plato.stanford.edu/entries/kant-aesthetics/#2

Statistic Brain. (2012, September 22). *Apple computer company statistics*. Retrieved 2013, from Statistic Brain: http://www.statisticbrain.com/apple-computer-company-statistics/

Stein, E. W. (2011). Improvisation as model for real-time decision-making. In F. Burstein, P. Brézillon, & A. Zaslavsky (Eds.), *Annals of information systems—Special volume in decision support systems: Supporting real time decision-making: The role of context in decision support on the move* (Vol. 13, pp. 13–34). Springer.

Stein, E., & Ahmad, N. (2009). Using the analytical hierarchy process (AHP) to construct a measure of the magnitude of consequences component of moral intensity. *Journal of Business Ethics 89*(3), 391–407.

Stein, E. W., Reychav, I., & Ben-Eliezer, D. (2014). *Assessing design thinking, behaviors and preferences in real and simulated world contexts*. (under review).

Strati, A. (1999). *Organization and aesthetics*. Thousand Oaks, CA: Sage.

Suzuki, S. (1970). *Zen mind, beginner's mind: Informal talks on zen meditation and practice*. Boston: Weatherhill.

Tuley, G. (2009). *Gever Tulley: Life lessons through tinkering*. Retrieved 2013, from ted.com: http://www.ted.com/talks/gever_tulley_s_tinkering_school_in_action.html

Webster's New World. (2010). *Webster's new world college dictionary*. New York, NY: John Wiley and Sons.

Weick, K. (1998). Improvisation as a mindset for organizational analysis. *Organization Science 9*(5), 543–555.

YCharts. (2013). *Cisco systems mart cap*. Retrieved October 16, 2013, from YCharts: http://ycharts.com/companies/CSCO/market_cap

Index

OTHER TITLES IN THE HUMAN RESOURCE MANAGEMENT AND ORGANIZATIONAL BEHAVIOR COLLECTION

Jean Phillips and Stan Gully, Rutgers University, Editors

- *Manage Your Career: 10 Keys to Survival and Success When Interviewing and On The Job* by Vijay Sathe
- *Culturally Intelligent Leadership: Leading Through Intercultural Interactions* by Mai Moua
- *Letting People Go: The People-Centered Approach to Firing and Laying Off Employees* by Matt Shlosberg
- *The Five Golden Rules of Negotiation* by Philippe Korda
- *Cross-Cultural Management* by Veronica Velo
- *Conversations About Job Performance: A Communication Perspective on the Appraisal Process* by Michael E. Gordon and Vernon Miller
- *How to Coach Individuals, Teams, and Organizations to Master Transformational Change Surfing Tsunamis* by Stephen K. Hacker
- *Managing Employee Turnover: Dispelling Myths and Fostering Evidence-Based Retention Strategies* by David Allen and Phil Bryant
- *Effective Interviewing and Information Gathering: Proven Tactics to Improve Your Questioning Skills* by Thomas Diamante
- *Essential Concepts of Cross-Cultural Management: Building on What We All Share* by Lawrence Beer
- *Growing Your Business: Making Human Resources Work for You* by Robert Baron
- *Developing Employee Talent to Perform: People Power* by Kim Warren

Announcing the Business Expert Press Digital Library

*Concise E-books Business Students Need
for Classroom and Research*

This book can also be purchased in an e-book collection by your library as
- a one-time purchase,
- that is owned forever,
- allows for simultaneous readers,
- has no restrictions on printing, and
- can be downloaded as PDFs from within the library community.

Our digital library collections are a great solution to beat the rising cost of textbooks. e-books can be loaded into their course management systems or onto student's e-book readers.

The **Business Expert Press** digital libraries are very affordable, with no obligation to buy in future years. For more information, please visit **www.businessexpertpress.com/librarians**. To set up a trial in the United States, please contact **Adam Chesler** at *adam.chesler@businessexpertpress.com* for all other regions, contact **Nicole Lee** at *nicole.lee@igroupnet.com*.

CPSIA information can be obtained at www.ICGtesting.com
Printed in the USA
BVOW08s2032120714

358845BV00004B/6/P